Red Thong Strong

"A funny, poignant read about friendships spanning three decades. These girlfriends share the stories, tips, how-tos, and memories that have made their lives richer, deeper, and more meaningful. You'll finish this book with eight new best friends!"
—Gina Spadafori, best-selling author

"Helpful, humorous, and an insightful exploration of what makes life and relationships work."
—Mary Tullie Critcher, author, *It's Greek to Me*

"A treasure trove of wit, wisdom, common sense advice and, yes, you have their permission to go ahead and wear a thong."
—Barbara Morris, R.Ph., editor, publisher, PutOldonHoldJournal.com

"A must for every woman's bookshelf....Lose yourself in this highly entertaining read and come out stronger."
—Darlene Arden, C.A.B.C., award-winning author, speaker, journalist

"I found myself nodding in agreement with the stories and snippets of wisdom passed along by the authors.... grab this book and look to it for sage advice about the importance of friendships."
—Ellen Jones, author, *The Healing Tree*

"A collection of delightful stories...Do yourself a favor and add *Red Thong Strong* to the top of your 'must-read' list. You can thank me later."

—Rebecca Nugent, author, *If the Devil Had a Wife*

"In today's world where books are a dime a dozen, this one is priceless!...It will give you all the tools you need to develop a strong relationship with your girlfriends."

—Donna Moss, designer, TV personality,
That's Haute boutique owner

"A perfect gift for those women in your life who you love and want to thank for their support and friendship. You will find yourself relating to the stories in the book while laughing and crying but most of all appreciating your friends."

—Dr. Annette Nolte, author and professor,
psychology and sociology

"*Red Thong Strong* is uniquely crafted by eight Texas girl-friends...Their faith in God comes through in an inspiring and humorous way."

—Dr. Eleanor Clark, award-winning author

"Reinforces...how important building strong friendships and having social support is to improving life's happiness!"

—Joe W. Rode, Ph.D., licensed professional counselor

"Every woman should read this…great advice for relationships with family and friends."
    —Jane Lee Jensen, author, *The Bull that Loved Bubblegum*

"Dig in. You'll love every single word. I did."
    —Susan B. Mead, best-selling author, *Dance with Jesus*

Terri Jutras

Charlotte Kei

Becky Elder

Dell Mann

Debbie Williams

Shelley Dejure

Debbi Comparin

Linda Storer

Red Thong Strong

Girlfriends' Little Secrets to Smoothing Life's Panty Lines

CHARLOTTE HILL • LINDA STORER
DEBBI COMPARIN • BECKY ELDER • TERRI JUTRAS
BEV MANN • SHELLEY TYLER • DEBBIE WILLIAMS

Cover and thong-a-tude illustrations by Courtney Allison Mohler

Photography by Rachel Klein

ISBN: 1517102960
ISBN 13: 9781517102968
Library of Congress Control Number: 2015914306
CreateSpace Independent Publishing Platform
North Charleston, South Carolina

This book is dedicated to Debbie Williams's insightful mother, Mildred Harder, for encouraging us to share our story.

We'd also like to dedicate it to our eight amazing husbands and eighteen loving children who unknowingly provided us with loads of material: you inspired us more than you know.

Contents

Red Thong Strong

Introduction

Get ready to trade in your granny panties for a bold, new attitude as we bare the secrets to becoming red thong strong. This thong-a-tude, as we call it, will inspire you to be smart, confident, and excited about life as you learn how to nurture your friendships and have your friendships nurture you.

We cooked up the idea for this book after wrapping up another successful party. We kicked off our stilettos, popped the cork on the Veuve champagne, and toasted each other. Reliving the evening's highlights, we realized what a good team we made. No surprise there—we'd worked and played together for decades.

Everyone from practical strangers to dear friends had been telling us we have something special: like Debbie's mom, who suggested we share our story. So then and there, we decided to do just that.

Some might have thought it would be challenging for a girlfriend group to write a book. But we were inspired. Tuesday night became our "book club" night—not for reading great works but for writing one. Picture a round table, dueling laptops, and eight opinionated women. Ideas flew as our typists, Charlotte and Linda, desperately tried to keep up. We added and subtracted words so many times it's a wonder this book was ever finished.

We debated, campaigned, and took sides, sharing high fives when we got our way and pouting when we didn't. It often felt like a tug-of-war, but the evening never ended with our panties in a wad!

With our help, you'll find yourself developing a little thong-a-tude in no time. There's always room for another friend at our table. So pull up a chair and meet the girls:

Charlotte—Smart, considerate, Olivia Newton-John lookalike, and breast cancer survivor with a thing for classic movies. Married in college. With her devoted husband, she formed the Sunday school class that made us family. Career focused, she was the last to have a child. Now a PR exec who blogs about her passions (fashion, beauty, and food) at Boomerbrief. com and our head writer.

Linda—Creative mastermind of our red thong strong philosophy. Longest married and eldest of the group, she's our "Mother Superior." This cupcake and champagne connoisseur is the ultimate event coordinator in both her personal and professional life. She inspires us to defy age and helps us fix everything from our hair to our homes.

Debbi—Down-to-earth deep thinker with a gift for seeing God in everyday situations. Easily mistaken for a teenager and readily identified by her infectious laugh. She married her college crush, like many of us, and was the first to start a family. This talented speaker now tutors young readers and writers.

Becky—Strong and spirited educator, lover of family, books, music, and exotic travel. A caring preacher's kid with a penchant for words who we've officially dubbed our grammar guru. She and her adventurous hubby are the only ones in our group to move from suburbia to urban living to a Texas hill country lake house.

Terri—Thoughtful caregiver who excels at psychoanalyzing others. Appears calm on the outside while often overwhelmed on the inside. Doctor's wife with four busy daughters who spends most of her time on call for her family and friends, near and far.

Bev—Witty, outgoing, Midwest farmer's daughter who married a traveling salesman. This former cheerleader still shakes her pom-poms whenever the Longhorns or Cowboys play. Keeps us in the know by sharing the latest tips and trends. The first girl to sport a thong and the last with her original hair color!

Shelley—High-energy, über-organized baby of the group. Talks faster than she can think! This child bride married her high school sweetheart at nineteen. Loves to exercise, scuba dive, and spend time with her grandchildren while still learning from her remarkable special-needs daughter.

Debbie—Shy, innocent Oklahoma country girl who fell for Big D and her future husband instantly. Our first mother of the bride and grandmother, this decorating diva often works out her visions in her dreams. Generous with her time and talents, she enjoys creating a warm, inviting home and helping others do the same.

1
Ridin' High

Thong-a-Tude
The small things behind the scenes are often what support us the most

"Oh my, that's so not you," Becky warned when Charlotte walked out in an outfit much bolder than her standard office attire.

"Sometimes you need to be someone other than you," said Linda, the acknowledged head of our band of sisters.

"Maybe it's me," Debbi volunteered. "Let me try it on for size."

"Charlotte, here's another top that's just what you need," offered Shelley.

The sun was shining as we celebrated a milestone birthday with a shopping expedition—much more than a mere trip with so many of us to dress. We helped and sometimes hindered each other's decisions, laughing as we occupied all the mirrors in the San Diego boutique. We were definitely causing a commotion—something we always seem to do when we're together!

In the midst of all the fun, an attractive, twentysomething woman standing nearby asked, "How many of you are there?"

"Eight," replied Debbie (not to be confused with Debbi), taking a breath from a deep conversation with Terri about their teenage daughters. "We've been friends forever."

"Yes, it's good to be here," Bev added. It was a comforting thought for our group of forty- to fifty-year-old friends, and one we were having more often lately.

"Oh, that's so nice." The onlooker sighed. "I wish I could be more like you. I only have one friend."

We were touched. After all, there's no higher compliment than the admiration of a younger woman. She noticed what we'd known for a long time: our group of friends is bound by something special. We call it "thong-a-tude," the little something underneath it all that keeps us together and gives us an edge.

—❧—

"Sometimes you need to be someone other than you." Linda

—❧—

Our Story

Faith brought us together more than thirty years ago. We found our church and then found our family of friends.

Our paths crossed in a young-marrieds' Sunday school class at Martin United Methodist Church in Bedford, Texas, a Dallas–Fort Worth suburb. We got acquainted while working in the nursery, planning fundraisers, and making playdates. Our friendship matured as our children did, eventually including parties, shopping trips, holiday gatherings, even family vacations. Now, there's not a single milestone in life that we do not celebrate together.

Our girlfriend group consists of eight dear friends. Inspired by the Red Hat Society's sisterhood and philosophy but wanting our own identity, we call ourselves Red Thong Strong or RTS. Between the two groups, both ends are covered!

The eight girls in our Red Thong Strong group include Debbi,
Shelley, Becky, Linda, Charlotte, Terri, Debbie, and Bev.

To us, the red thong symbolizes freedom. We've lost a lot of our inhibitions; we're bolder, more assertive, and more sure of ourselves. Today, we try things we might have shied away from in the past, things that keep us young. We run marathons, hike, bike, parasail, travel, dance, go to concerts, start our own businesses, and change hairstylists often. We reinvent ourselves constantly and embrace change!

Our girlfriends encourage, inspire, and support us. We don't just enjoy each other's company; we require it...almost as much as our Diet Coke and Starbucks Skinny Vanilla Latte.

"God put our group together. We just showed up
and paid attention." Shelley

What Makes Our Girlfriends so Special?

We are eight women bound together by the belief that our friendship makes life richer. Each of us has unique gifts and contributes a special something to the group:

- Charlotte, our boardroom babe, blends business savvy and compassion to motivate and inspire us.
- Linda, our personal stylist, wows us with her spot-on fashion sense but rarely saves us cents.
- Debbi, our spiritual leader, guides us in the right direction and sells us on life's best.
- Becky, our travel and trivia expert, reminds us of who we are, what we've seen, and where we're headed.
- Terri, our unofficial psychologist, combines *Cosmo* and *Guideposts* to help us solve our issues.
- Bev, our domestic diva, keeps us current. She's HGTV, Food Network, and Fox News rolled into one.
- Shelley, our personal trainer and life coach, encourages us to reach our goals.
- Debbie, our goodwill ambassador, urges us to listen, love, and look for the positive.

All these special somethings have blended together over the years and formed forever friendships. We provide each other a safe place to laugh, cry, complain, moan, worry, commiserate, pray, and ultimately rejoice! When you're this blessed, you have to share your good fortune with others.

"Who needs plain vanilla when you can have rocky road?" Becky

Time before Girlfriends

Consider Eve. There she was in the Garden of Eden with only Adam to talk to, and of course, he was too busy hanging out in his man cave. Eve was feeling lonely and neglected. If she'd had our group of girlfriends, things might have gone differently:

Charlotte would've empathized…

> "I know you're lonely, but talkin' to that snake is no solution. Let's put our heads together and make him hiss-tory."

Linda would've instructed…

> "Listen, girlfriend, that ol' serpent is no fashionista. Au naturel is definitely your look."

Debbi would've counseled…

> "You need to keep focused, focused, focused, and when temptation comes your way, stop and pray, pray, pray."

Becky would've suggested…

> "Eve, let's talk. A change of scenery could do you good, so let's plan a girl's getaway."

Terri would've advised…

> "Girlfriend, do not eat that fruit from the tree. If you do, we'll always have to worry about what we look like in our bathing suits."

Bev would've directed…

> "Eve, scratch the apple pie. If you want Adam to stay healthy, go with a fresh garden salad instead."

Shelley would've shouted…

> "Girl, you're not thinking straight. You need to train for the marathon ahead, so you can outrun those who want to make you stumble."

Debbie would've scolded…

> "Honey, I just cleaned the Garden. Are you sure you want to mess things up by eating that apple?"

Eve certainly needed some soul sisters to talk to before taking that eye-opening bite of apple!

Girlfriends keep girlfriends accountable. When we need encouragement, they help us along the way. Between the eight of us, we always have someone to turn to for advice. The close-knit friendship at our core supports and sustains us.

"Surrounding yourself with soul sisters can be life changing." Debbie

2
Finding That Perfect Fit

Thong-a-Tude
It takes time to find something flattering and forgiving.

We've seen many changes the last thirty years. In the '80s, we were the queens of big Texas hair and Linda Evans's shoulder pads. Becky introduced us to Units clothing. Terri sold us on matching Christmas sweatshirts and big paper-mache earrings. Debbi got us hooked on Mexican muumuus, and Linda told us when it was time to move on to the next trend.

Debbie, Debbi, Linda, and Charlotte show off their '80s' style.

Today, we pay big bucks for brazilian blowouts and the perfect skinny jeans. Bev shows us how to change our look by simply adding a scarf or two. Debbie helps us kick it up a notch with sexy stilettos and wild animal prints. Shelley convinces us to invest in designer bags, the bigger the better. And Charlotte urges us to accent with a menagerie of belts, necklaces, and bracelets. Meanwhile, thongs have gone from our feet to our fannies!

Over the years, fashions have come and gone, but our friendships have remained constant. What are the threads that have held us together? Our little secrets will help you find and keep friends for life.

Love Yourself

Before developing relationships with others, you have to take care of you. Put yourself at the top of your to-do list. Take a few minutes each day for things you enjoy: read a devotional, take a walk, catch up on your favorite Netflix series, or connect with Facebook friends. You have to give to yourself before you can give to others.

Remember the "Calgon, take me away" commercials? Terri escapes by locking the bathroom door, lighting candles, and taking bubble baths. That's when she does some of her best thinking. When her children were young, she would steal away for a moment of solitude while her girls slid notes under the bathroom door. She may have only been there for five minutes, but it was time well spent. Afterward, she felt refreshed and ready to handle anything.

When you take time for yourself, frustrations dissolve. All you need is a moment.

"You have to give to yourself before you can give to others." Bev

Make Time

Friendships take effort. Although life can be busy, you need to schedule time to be with friends. Have lunch, go shopping, walk and talk, make an impromptu call, celebrate birthdays, and plan things that make your friends feel special. Our husbands say we meet any time someone starts her period…any excuse for a party! When we get together, we always end with a hug and ask, "When can we meet again?"

One of our favorite together times is our annual Christmas getaway to a Texas bed-and-breakfast. We always schedule it around the Holiday Stroll, the second weekend in December.

A few years ago, Debbie and Becky were feeling particularly stressed about fitting in the trip. They'd committed but began to regret the decision because they were so overwhelmed. They needed to wrap presents, plan office parties, decorate their trees, and complete countless other holiday tasks. Then again, they didn't want to miss out on all the fun and fellowship.

Jokingly, Becky reminded Debbie "We have to go…or they'll talk about us!"

They forgot their worries as soon as they hit the road. Three hours later, we were all laughing, shopping, and sipping champagne. Getting together eased all our holiday anxieties and filled us with the true Christmas spirit.

*Our carriage driver, Becky, Linda, Charlotte, Debbi, Debbie,
Bev, and Shelley welcome the holidays in Granbury, TX.*

Our hectic lives make it difficult to focus on friendships. But if
you make the time, you will be richly rewarded.

*"Our husbands say we meet anytime someone starts
her period…any excuse for a party!" Charlotte*

Jump Right In

You can find friends anywhere: your neighborhood, work, yoga,
Starbucks, or church…where we found each other. You just have
to keep your eyes open to possibilities.

Friendship requires action. To make a friend, you have to be a friend. Volunteer in the nursery, take a meal, make a play-date, offer to carpool, send a card, or invite your neighbor for wine—just be spontaneous. Bev is a great one for picking up the phone to see if any of us needs something while she runs errands. Debbie enjoys surprising us with cheery bouquets for no reason. Friendship isn't a spectator sport; you must participate.

When Linda joined our Sunday school class, Terri eyed her accessories and immediately recognized a fellow fashion fanatic. She couldn't wait to call Linda to find out where she shopped. During the conversation, they discovered they both had daughters, their husbands were often MIA, and they loved shoes. Terri jumped right in and invited Linda out for lunch and shopping.

They had so much fun they lost track of time. Linda needed to call home to tell the sitter they were going to be late. Since this was pre–cell phone era, they had to pull over and use a public pay phone.

Before Linda made her call, she took out her Kleenex and carefully covered the entire receiver. Terri watched in amazement, realizing she and Linda had something else in common. They were both germophobes!

Terri's reaching out gave birth to a beautiful friendship. That simple phone call led to a thirty-plus-year bond. Sometimes you have to take a chance and jump right in.

~ co

"Friendship isn't a spectator sport; you must participate." Debbi

~ co

Lighten Up–and We Don't Mean Your Hair!

No relationship is perfect. You have to let some things roll off your back. In any group, you will encounter off-the-cuff remarks that aren't intended to hurt feelings but can if taken too personally. Blow it off! You know things aren't always about you. You can't always make biscuits that are light and fluffy. You're not always going to have a good hair day. You're not always going to be on time. But don't let an insensitive remark or action spoil your fun.

Take, for example, the dinner party at Bev's house. Since Martha Stewart was incarcerated at the time, Bev felt the need to fill the void. She spent days cleaning house, polishing silver, and cooking a five-course meal complete with fresh herbs snipped from her garden. Being her mother's daughter, everything came from scratch—even her croutons were homemade. This would be no ordinary meal.

Imagine Bev's surprise when Shelley arrived at the door with a Ziploc bag of raw vegetables. A health and fitness enthusiast, Shelley was only forty-eight hours from completing an intensive twenty-one-day food detox. She had brought her own dinner because she didn't want to be tempted to break her program.

Tension filled the air. Bev's first instinct was to turn and walk away. But after a moment, she invited Shelley inside, saying, "Hey, if everyone had brought something like this, I wouldn't have had to cook."

On entering the kitchen, Shelley realized all the effort that had gone into planning the event, decided to forgo her regimen, and went straight for the parmesan crisps.

Meeting in the middle helped Bev and Shelley avoid hurt feelings and an uncomfortable situation that could've ruined the night for our entire group. By lightening up, they turned those vegetables into a wonderful gazpacho, which led to an evening of delicious food and delightful conversation.

Life is too short to waste stewing over imagined criticism. Instead, take a deep breath before you react and look in the mirror. Ask yourself the following questions:

- Have my hormones hijacked my emotions?
- Am I stressed out, overworked, or just being a drama queen?
- Will I feel better if I turn the other cheek?

If the answer is yes, you know what to do. Smile, lighten up, and let it go so you can mend and move on.

⁓

"If things aren't going your way, don't get your thong in a tangle!" Debbie

⁓

Laugh Out Loud

People are drawn to laughter. This stress-busting medicine heals, rejuvenates, and helps us bond.

We laugh together, laugh at each other, and laugh at ourselves. We know we aren't perfect (even though we try hard to be!). Charlotte can be fashion challenged; Shelley, Debbie, and Becky are cooking impaired; Linda doesn't know how to be casual; and Debbi can spend what seems like days deciding on a pair of house slippers (or sunglasses or an umbrella or jewelry...). But together, we embrace our shortcomings and laugh them off.

Charlotte is almost perfect in every way. A petite blue-eyed blond, she has a sweet, soothing personality. On the other hand, she is an assertive public relations exec who writes a successful baby boomer blog with her husband, Bob.

We were on one of our group shopping expeditions, and Charlotte found something that caught her eye. After what seemed like hours in the dressing room, we asked, "Charlotte, are you OK?"

She didn't answer immediately. When Charlotte finally emerged, she hesitantly modeled the top, saying, "I can't figure out why this thing doesn't fit. What's wrong?"

Our fashion advisor, Linda stepped up, trying her best to suppress her giggles. "Charlotte, you have it on backward!"

We howled. She had put the top on wrong, and the pocket was on her shoulder!

Charlotte did buy that top, and it looked beautiful worn the right way. But to this day, we can't help chuckling when she enters a dressing room.

Wherever we go, our contagious laughter seems to cause a commotion. We have so much fun others want to join in.

Welcome the good times, share the joy, and watch the door to new friendships swing wide open.

—❧—

"Who needs perfection? Talk about boring." Linda

—❧—

Bare Yourself

Confiding in others can be therapeutic. Begin by discussing the good things happening in your life: a new baby, your paleo diet success, your daughter's cheerleading tryouts, your son's first solo, or the shoes you have your eye on at Nordstrom.

As your friendship grows, you'll become more comfortable sharing concerns. Soon, it'll be easier to open up, peeling back the guarded layers to your heart and soul.

Baring yourself is a scary thought but can be just what the doctor ordered.

Before thongs were trendy, Bev forged ahead of us by sporting the new undergarment. A beautiful lady with naturally blond hair, she was quite proud to be on the cutting edge of fashion. Thongs became a part of her daily wardrobe. She wore them everywhere—even to a dermatologist appointment. After all, he would be examining only her face (or so she thought...).

A fair-skinned sun-worshipper, Bev was concerned about spots on her face and neck. The doctor took one look at her complexion and decided a full-body check was in order. He told her to undress to her bra and panties. Realizing the revealing nature of her unmentionables, Bev started to make excuses for a quick exit. The dermatologist, however, assured her the examination would take no time at all.

When he stepped out for her to undress, Bev frantically searched the room for something to wrap around her exposed backside!

Unfortunately, nothing could remedy the embarrassing situation, so she was forced to show her bare behind when he returned.

As Bev prepared for the worst, the doctor surprised her by saying, "Oh, I bought my wife some of those, but she won't wear them."

Though her cheeks turned red, Bev was quite relieved at his nonchalance. His comments put her at ease and gave her a story that always makes us laugh until we cry.

The thought of baring yourself to new friends can be just as uncomfortable as Bev's dermatologist visit. But sharing your joys and worries with someone you trust can deepen the relationship and create a lasting bond.

We've turned to each other for guidance and wisdom as our kids have gone from diapers to diplomas. The advice we received wasn't always what we *wanted* to hear, but more often than not, it was what we *needed* to hear. Knowing that someone understands, accepts, and loves you for who you are provides tremendous comfort. When you reach this level of friendship, soul sisters are born.

"When we meet, we always take time to bare it."
Terri

Show Support

Everyone goes through difficult times. We've experienced job changes, births of new businesses, life-threatening illnesses, surgeries, losses of loved ones, and ongoing support of a special-needs child.

What can *you* do to help someone going through a tough time? Listen with more than your ears, use your heart, and notice body language. Don't wait for a call or you could miss an opportunity to be a blessing in someone else's life. Instead, anticipate needs and make the first move.

We've found the little things mean the most, not the big showy gestures. Whether you send a card, bring a casserole, sit with a friend in a hospital waiting room, or simply listen, you are providing support. You can make a difference.

> *Shelley's family had been going to Martin Methodist for a little more than a year when her second daughter, Mallory, was born. Hours after delivery, they learned she might have Down syndrome.*

> *Life became a blur of tears and fears for the next three weeks as the family anxiously awaited test results. Although worried beyond belief, Shelley and her husband, Gene, did their best to keep things "normal" for their four-year-old daughter, Lindsey. They were in unknown territory and didn't want to add anxiety by sharing too much.*

Mallory experienced severe breathing problems and had to be rushed to the hospital during this agonizing waiting period. While she was having life-saving surgery, big sister Lindsey entered a crisis of her own. Sensing that something was terribly wrong, she withdrew from the family and stopped eating. Her eyes began to cross. Two specialists and an MRI ruled out a brain tumor and revealed a virus had attacked Lindsey's optic nerve, causing her eye issues.

When this news was announced in Sunday school, Debbi made it a point to call Shelley and offer help. Knowing Mallory required constant attention, Debbi suggested a playdate.

"You're a lifesaver," Shelley said. "Lindsey would love spending time with your kids!"

Next thing Debbi knew, her kitchen table resembled a Hobby Lobby craft class. Seven-year-old MaryAnn was busy teaching Lindsey and little sister Angelina how to make colorful potholders and friendship bracelets. Screams of laughter rang through the house when three-year-old Joseph joined the mix and sent the stretchy yarn flying.

Returning home after a fun-filled afternoon, Lindsey was all smiles. She proudly showed off her creations *while chattering nonstop. Shelley's heart warmed, seeing her daughter return to her happy self. The time spent with her new friends had certainly boosted Lindsey's spirits.*

Debbi had no idea her phone call would have such an impact. Even a small show of support can lift someone emotionally, connect you both spiritually, and provide strength to meet challenges. Facing tough times together can also give a friendship roots.

Thanks to Debbi's show of support, Angelina, Lindsey, MaryAnn, Mallory, and Joseph became great friends.

Fast-forward eighteen years, and we find Shelley's and Debbi's families closer than ever. At Lindsey's wedding, a beautiful, healthy Mallory shared the spotlight as her sister's maid of honor. And Joe? He almost stole the show by agreeing to stand up with Lindsey as a "bridesman."

"You can make a difference. One small act of kindness can mean more than a thousand words." Shelley

Accept Kindness

When a friend shows you kindness, welcome and treasure it. Your first impulse might be to reject all offers because you're worried about putting people out, being a burden, or losing control.

After all, as women, we strive to be perfect and self-sufficient. Accepting help may go against your nature, but don't think of it as a sign of weakness.

As a public relations executive, Charlotte makes countless decisions every day. Because of the demands of her job, she has organized her life to a fault. She follows a strict meal planning regimen: shopping on Friday, cooking on Saturday, labeling and freezing meals on Sunday, then posting a printout of the freezer's inventory on her refrigerator.

This worked well until her husband Bob's unexpected health crisis threw a kink in her routine. She had to single-handedly manage the family-owned business, help him through surgery and rehab, and still be there for their teenage son, Cole. Taking on the role of Wonder Woman, she rejected all offers of help.

Of course, her stubborn friends ignored her refusals. On a cold December day when Charlotte was feeling as dreary as the weather, the doorbell rang. There stood Linda with a pot of comforting chicken noodle soup. Moments later, Bev and Terri arrived with a delicious pork roast and creamy mashed potatoes. Shelley and Debbi completed the surprise with chicken spaghetti and homemade apple pie. In no time, they had the makings of an old-fashioned Methodist covered-dish supper.

By opening the door, Charlotte accepted more than just food. She welcomed kindness and realized she didn't have to face the situation alone.

Charlotte learned a valuable lesson that day. If you are faced with trying times, let your friends help.

_⤜ꝏ_

"Sometimes you have to hang up the Wonder
Woman cape, accept kindness, and lean on others."
Charlotte

_⤜ꝏ_

Collect Memories

While writing this book, we've reflected on our friendship and
relived decades of memories. Some of our recollections are tender
times, many are side-splitting, hysterical, Diet Coke-coming-
out-of-your-nose moments, and others are spiritual journeys
where we held hands and prayed together. But they all have one
thing in common—they brought us closer.

Anytime you're with friends, you have a chance to make a
memory, so take plenty of selfies. If you're like us, writing
things down also helps, so you don't forget. You create memories when you shop together, celebrate birthdays, travel, or just
meet for lunch. Even sitting in the airport can be a memory
moment…

> *After an unforgettable trip for Debbi's fiftieth birthday, we
> were sitting in the San Diego airport waiting for our return
> flight home. Wanting to remember every detail (at fifty—
> the memory isn't what it used to be), Debbi started grabbing*

any available sheet of paper: a leftover napkin, her boarding pass, a bank deposit slip…anything she could get her hands on to record this special occasion.

Soon, we were reliving our trip and laughing uncontrollably at our escapades as Debbi wrote frantically. We were causing such a commotion that others waiting for the flight wanted to join us.

"What's the occasion?" a young man asked. "You girls are just having too much fun."

Shelley, Terri, Charlotte, Debbi, Linda, and Becky celebrate Debbi's fiftieth birthday in San Diego.

"We've been celebrating her birthday," Terri said pointing at Debbi. "Can you believe she's fifty?" He looked at Debbi in amazement, and said "Wow! I hope my wife looks that good at your age."

Talk about an ego boost! Debbi may have blushed but we beamed, knowing that comment was the icing on her birthday cake.

Before long, it felt like a party. Almost everyone at Gate 10 was laughing with us. From start to finish, this milestone celebration was one for the books.

Time spent with friends is priceless, so, be mindful of those moments. Stop rushing through things and start collecting memories.

─⸲─

"Anytime you're with friends is a chance to make a memory." Becky

─⸲─

We hope the tips in this chapter will help you find girlfriends who fit you perfectly. Just remember, making friends is a process that requires time and action. Step out of your comfort zone and get involved. You might just create soul sisters for life and collect memories along the way.

Sizing Up Soul Sisters

Cherish friends who

Share everything from shoes to salads
Open up to you
Understand your moods
Laugh at imperfections

Stay young at heart
Insist on time together
Shoulder your burdens
Tell you the truth
Encourage you
Remember all your stories and laugh every time

3
Smoothing Life's Wrinkles

Thong-a-Tude
Relationships can provide a much-needed boost or give you wedgies.
But they're worth the effort!

So much to do...so little time.

Picture this—your alarm clock rings, and you hit the floor running, realizing you're already behind schedule. Frazzled and frustrated? Well, hold on. You'll feel better in a minute. Girlfriends can come to your rescue.

We work hard to make all aspects of our lives run smoothly. In today's busy world, we're stretched in many different directions.

Multitasking is second nature as we move from baker to bus driver in the morning and secretary to sex goddess at night.

Friends can help friends. With a strong social network, you can count on someone being there to assist you in smoothing life's wrinkles. In our thong squad, we all have specialties. Shelley lifts us up when we're feeling sad or depressed. Terri has incredible insight when it comes to relationships. And we've all turned to Debbi for support when our kids are driving us crazy. Together, we solve everything from headaches to heartaches.

Being Comfortable in Your Own Skin

Girlfriends help you feel better about yourself. It can be like having your own personal therapist 24/7, free of charge. They offer the perfect prescription by doing the following:

Listening—One of the most important things you can do as a girlfriend is to listen. Often, a friend just needs to let off steam to someone who cares as a release. You don't have to say anything. In fact, sometimes, it's better if you don't.

Empathizing—Women relate to women, so empathizing comes naturally. We feel each other's joys and pains. Friends identify with what we're going through, bringing comfort because they've often been there too. You show empathy by laughing and crying together. Your husband may not get your issues when your hair turns orange after a bad highlighting, but your girlfriends will.

Speaking—We all need encouragement. Your words of support can help validate another's feelings, lift her up, and help her realize she's not alone. Besides making her feel better, knowing someone really cares will empower her. So speak up. Sincere praise, compliments, and kind words can be life changing.

Touching—We're all hungry for meaningful contact. In fact, a UCLA study* found that everyone needs eight to ten meaningful touches daily just to maintain their emotional and physical health. Touching can be for more than greetings and goodbyes. The healing power in a pat, a squeeze on the arm, or a hug benefits both the giver and the receiver. A touch can give you an emotional connection, warm a friend's heart, and let her know she's accepted and loved.

Laughing—Laughing out loud is therapeutic. It relieves stress, minimizes problems, refreshes you, and even better, keeps you looking younger. We all need to laugh more. Research shows adults laugh only about fifteen times per day while children laugh four hundred times a day. Close the gap by finding your inner child. It's healthy to laugh at yourself and with friends. So giggle, chuckle, snicker, or snort, but always leave 'em laughing.

---

* UCLA Monthly, *Alumni Association News*, March - April 1981: 1.

Whether you have a heavy heart or you're just having a harried day, these loving actions can boost your mental health. We routinely use this prescription in our relationship therapy sessions, where we take time to listen to each other.

"Your husband may not get your issues when your hair turns orange, but your girlfriends will." Terri

We empathize when Linda recounts her stressful workday. We encourage Shelley and pass out hugs when she worries about her upcoming surgery. Then Bev lightens the mood with a witty comment, and we dissolve into laughter. These cure-alls strengthen our friendship and help us feel comfortable in our own skins.

Avoiding Side Effects

Encourage open discussions by practicing the following:

Respect—Follow the Golden Rule by doing unto others as you would have them do unto you.

Timing—Listen, watch for an invitation, and respond on cue.

Sensitivity—Remember that what happens in RTS, stays in RTS, and your friendship will stay true.

Living with Boxers

We all know men are from Mars. So whether they wear boxers or briefs, we need help understanding them. Girlfriends provide a sympathetic ear that keeps us from becoming desperate housewives.

Boxers versus Thongs

Women need their girlfriends like men need their remote controls. Give a man an electronic gadget that doesn't talk back, and he's in heaven! Men have friends to play golf or poker with, but they seldom pick up the phone just to talk. Actually, men are capable of only about 1,500 words a day, and it seems they use 1,499 of them at work.

Women, on the other hand, have a capacity of about a million words a day. We talk at length with our girlfriends, covering topics from A to Z.

A—"I found the cutest ankle booties today!" Linda
to
Z—"What's wrong with this picture? How can I have zits *and* wrinkles?" Becky

Men are brief and to the point when they leave voice mail: *"Hey, this is Tony…give me a call."*

While women go on and on…

"Hi Becky, this is Linda. Sorry to call so early, I'm sure you're taking a walk.

I just got back from the grocery store and forgot to get that recipe we talked about the other day. We're having a luncheon at work this week, and I'd like to take that dish. So please, please, call me when you have a chance.

Also, let's talk about this weekend and the plans for our next get-together. You know, we need to celebrate Shelley's birthday next month, and we might want to get a jump start and think about that, too. I hope Blake's feeling better. Talk to you soon. Bye."

Women not only like to talk, we want details. We need to know who, what, when, where, how, and why about everything. For example, when Debbie comes in wearing a new pair of shoes, we all want the scoop: "Where did you get them? Who did you go with? How much did they cost? Do they come in a different color? Can I try them on?"

Women enjoy dealing with emotions. We live to socialize and sympathize. We want to feel. When Charlotte and Bob go to the library for DVDs, they usually turn in opposite directions. Charlotte gravitates toward romantic (and sometimes sappy) tearjerkers like *When Harry Met Sally* while Bob heads straight to mindless comedies like *Anchorman*. Most men aren't interested in movies with feelings unless, of course, they include sex.

Speaking of sex…now, that's a hot topic. Men always seem to be interested in sex no matter what. And when we don't have a headache, we enjoy it too.

After all during sex, you have your husband's total attention, and you're reminded how good you are together. Then reality returns. You're in the mood to cuddle, but he's already turned on ESPN to catch the last of the basketball game.

It will always be Mars versus Venus, testosterone versus estrogen, and of course, boxers versus thongs.

—∽

"Women need their girlfriends like men need their remote controls," Debbi

—∽

The Skinny on Handling Boxers

Whether your man wears boxers, prefers tighty-whities, or goes commando, you sometimes need to handle him with care. When that doesn't come naturally, girlfriends can help you turn the situation right side out.

We share, compare, and air our dirty laundry in RTS discussions devoted to dealing with men. We're amazed we ever finished this book because some nights we spent more time in therapy than writing.

You can always tell when a girlfriend has an issue. With eight of us, someone usually needs to vent to avoid hanging her man out to dry.

At a particular meeting, one girlfriend came in late (we're not naming names because what happens in RTS stays in RTS). The slamming door was our first clue that there was trouble in paradise or, in this instance, bedlam in Bedford. It was obviously a case of thongs versus boxers.

Expecting the worst, we asked for details. As she unloaded, we learned the problem centered on a misunderstanding about picking up dry cleaning for an important business trip. We were immediately sympathetic, validating her feelings. We'd all been there before—if not with dry cleaning, with something similar—and we shared our own experiences. (You can tell this writing session was a wash.)

Using us as a sounding board, she sorted through her frustrations, and we helped iron out the problem. Together, we diffused what could've been a volatile situation. Crisis avoided! In the end, our intervention softened her anger, so she could send him off on his trip with a hug and kiss.

Since men don't come with instructions, we rely on friends to help keep our relationships from going down the drain. We handle our boxers like we do our delicates—with care—using the gentle cycle.

⎯⎯ᗧ

"Don't put your boxers through the wringer." Bev

⎯⎯ᗧ

Surviving Relationship Wear and Tear

We love our boxers, and taking care of them has helped us enjoy lasting relationships. We're all fortunate to have been married for more than thirty years, and we're each still on our first husbands! It hasn't all been a bed of roses—no marriage is perfect.

The fabric of a relationship changes both physically and emotionally as we go through life's cycles. In the beginning, you work to show your best side. As things heat up, you have "the conversation" and start shopping rings. Next thing you know, you're married with children, and responsibility takes over. Consumed with the demands of a career and growing family, you must make an effort to connect with each other. The more time you invest, the greater the rewards. As the years go by, other couples may drift apart, but your love and friendship will deepen.

We should know...we've stayed together a combined three hundred-plus years of marriage. How've we done it? Although at times our lives have spun out of control, we've relied on our girlfriend group to share the heaviest loads. The more we share, the more we learn, and the closer we become. Along the way, we've picked up these tips for keeping our marital relationships in balance:

Put Each Other First—Set aside time to be together. Get off the smartphone and stop folding clothes. If you want to turn him on, turn everything else off and give him your undivided attention.

Appreciate the Little Things—Simple surprises can make your relationship sparkle. You know you're loved when he makes the bed (even with the twenty tasseled and feathered pillows), fixes your coffee just how you like it while you're getting ready, and plans date night around the chick flick you've been wanting to see.

Express Yourself—If you love him truly, madly, deeply, tell him. Begin the day with a hug and kiss, and then welcome each other home. Say "I love you" and say it often. No one can hear it enough.

Take Comfort in the Routine—Forget traditional roles. Work as a team, and divvy up the duties. Dad may make the pancakes while Mom manages the money. Share everything from housework to yard work.

Keep Your Promises—Don't take the easy way out. Stick with it, and remember, you're in this together. Deal with problems head on instead of running away. If you walk out the door when times get rough, you might not be followed.

Enjoy Doing Your Own Thing—Don't make your spouse your hobby. You should share some common interests (other than your children), but you also need your own space. Work out, garden, or spend time with your girlfriends—like we do—while your husband goes hunting.

Debbi, Charlotte, Linda, Becky, and Terri enjoy girl time while their guys play golf in the '80s.

Have Adjustable Expectations— Just roll with it. Remember, this is reality, not a storybook romance. He may not be Richard Gere, but you're probably not Julia Roberts. So be content with each other. Contentment leads to happiness.

Connect with Other Couples—Girls and their guys just want to have fun. Spending time with other couples is one of our favorite things. Together, we enjoy dinners, concerts, and traveling, complete with lively, thought-provoking conversation. These times strengthen and bond both our friendships and our marriages.

Seek Guidance—When a pipe breaks, you call a plumber. So, why do we hesitate to ask for help when our marriages need it? Every relationship has highs and lows. When the inevitable happens, don't keep it to yourself. You don't have to shoulder the burden alone. Turn to a close friend, your pastor, or a counselor for help.

Keep the Romance Alive—Never stop dating. Saying "I do" doesn't mean you can stop the courtship. Start on day one and continue when you have kids. Splurge on a babysitter and plan special time together. Everybody benefits. The kids won't be so dependent, and your marriage will be renewed. You'll continue to learn about each other and stay connected.

Remember the power of passion. You can recapture that original spark if you use your imagination. Having trouble? Our pointers will give your romance a jump start.

Nine Passion Pointers

1. **Ditch the distractions**—To get his full attention, lose the laptop, turn off the TV, and disable the doorbell.
2. **Set the stage**—Chill the prosecco, put on some Michael Bublé, light plenty of candles, and splash on a seductive scent. Call your honey's name, and he'll come running.
3. **Keep him guessing**—Do something unexpected and fun, like running a scented bubble bath for two in the middle of the afternoon.
4. **Compliment your guy**—Stretch the truth. Sometimes a little white lie does more than "the little blue pill."
5. **Seize the moment**—Foreplay can start in the kitchen and follow you into the bedroom.
6. **Get physical**—Surprise him with a gentle touch or kiss. You won't believe the response you'll get if you're the initiator.

7. **Spend the night out**—Whether you book the Holiday Inn or the Hyatt, hotel sex does wonders for your relationship.

8. **Think thong**—It's hard to set the mood in flannel pajamas, granny panties, and slipper socks. You have to *feel* sexy before you can *be* sexy.

9. **Take a second honeymoon**—And a third and a fourth! Surprising him with packed bags and a secret destination can be just the ticket to keeping the romance alive.

⌐

"If you want to turn him on, turn everything else off and give him your undivided attention."
Charlotte

⌐

Taking Kids from Diapers to Diplomas
Fasten your seatbelt and get ready for the ride of your life.

Raising children is like taking a road trip. It helps to chart a course and consult those who've been there before. Experienced travelers can help you navigate rough roads and avoid the potholes of parenting. But no matter how much you prepare, you're going to run into unexpected hazards. Then, instead of calling AAA, we call RTS.

Our friends have helped us manage everything from potty training to driver's ed. We're living proof that it takes a village to raise a child. Together, we've nurtured eighteen babies, and we continue to consult each other as we move from mother to mentor.

Here are some tips we've collected on this journey called parenthood:

Dealing with Diapers

These years are not for the faint-hearted. Your whole world changes when they place your first child in your arms. This cute little bundle of joy may look helpless, but this baby will dictate your life…when you sleep, eat, shower.

You watch every move, hypersensitive to each sneeze, rash, and hiccup. You wonder, "Is this something serious or is this what every baby does?" You need an expert. Friends can help, especially if your family isn't nearby, or if you're not ready for one of grandma's home remedies. *What the heck is a "sugar tit" anyway?*

Thank goodness our friend Debbi blazed the motherhood trail. We called her day and night for emergency crib-side assistance on everything from what diapers to buy and when to start cereal to how to use a rectal thermometer; then we moved on to who's the best pediatrician, where to sign up for mother's day out, and why museum school is a must.

Together, we discovered you don't have to do everything by the book:

- Cloth diapers don't necessarily make you a better mother.
- You can buy the most expensive toys, but your child will still go for the box and ribbon.
- There's no harm in giving Little Tikes kitchens to boys or Tonka trucks to girls.
- A late-afternoon dip in the wading pool can count as a bath.
- It's OK to let your children pick out their own clothes—even if they don't match.
- All children walk, talk, and use the potty on their own schedule.

Childhood is not a checklist or a competition. You'll never pass this way again. Enjoy the ride.

—❧

"What the heck is a 'sugar tit' anyway?" Debbi

—❧

Driving Miss Crazy
Start your engine.

The taxicab years begin as soon as your child becomes involved in his first activity: T-ball, gymnastics, swimming lessons—we tried them all. Between practices and games, we've logged more miles than the space shuttle. Too bad they don't have a reward system for frequent drivers.

The car becomes multifunctional, serving as restaurant, dressing room, and study hall. If you have more than one child, your only hope for survival is to carpool. Again, girlfriends can come to the rescue. They can help solve your driving dilemmas, especially if your children are in the same activities. This is also a great time to meet other moms. Just ask Bev. She made many new friends while watching her sons, Tommy and Dusty, play football.

During this race-and-chase stage, organization was the key to our sanity. Shelley made sure Mallory's backpack was prepared and by the backdoor the night before. Together, they did homework, made lunches, and set out clothes for the next day. Linda, the queen of lists, posted reminders of appointments, practices, and projects on the bathroom mirror. Debbie used index cards for tomorrow's to-dos, putting them in the order they needed to be completed. We each had a system that worked.

How can you avoid becoming a "mad mom on a mission"?

Just say no—An overbooked schedule means an overstressed life.

Ask for help—You don't have to do it all on your own.

Label, label, label—Don't let Jonathan wind up at baseball with Emily's dance bag.

Cut the whining—Teach yourself and your children to be flexible.

Focus on Friday—The weekend *will* come eventually.

This can be one of the busiest times of your life. Embrace these years that keep you behind the wheel. You won't always have this much control.

—◦

"Don't leave your fundraiser candy bars in the car on a hot August day. They will melt." Bev

—◦

Dating, Doubts, and Decisions
Caution: Rough terrain ahead.

This time of cheers, fears, tears, and plenty of prayers comes just when you hoped to shift into cruise. You must be alert and fully prepared for the bumps and curves ahead as puberty kicks in.

Hormones rule. Hair starts appearing in odd places, and overnight, your child becomes an alien. Acne, braces, and embarrassing locker room situations are common. Girls turn into drama queens while boys retreat to their caves. Frustration sets in, and your new teenager takes it out on you.

Boarding school begins to look like a good idea when they exert their independence. Real battles break out as they try body piercings, tattoos, and wild hair colors. Your little rebel may ignore curfews, date the person you'd least expect, and hang out with questionable characters. You worry about anything and everything a teenager could possibly get into: smoking, alcohol, drugs, driving, and s-e-x (not necessarily in that order).

But hang on through their highs and lows, and eventually, you both will make it. The key is to love them through it, pray persistently, and lean on your friends for support. You can take comfort in knowing you aren't alone. Should a crash occur, your girlfriends can be the airbags that cushion the impact.

Remember these tips when traveling this rocky road:

Lend an ear—Listen to your children today, and they'll listen to you tomorrow.

Keep your eyes open—Know who your kids hang out with, where they're going, and what they're doing.

Communicate limits—Teenagers need and want boundaries (although they'll never admit it!).

Choose your battles—Decide what you absolutely will not tolerate and roll with the rest.

Take a stand—It may be one of the hardest things you'll do, but step up and *be* a parent...not their best friend.

You'll need stamina and perseverance to fuel this emotional stage. Keep your eyes fixed on the road ahead and forget bailing out. You're in this for the long haul.

~⑤~

"Keep an eye on your worry meter. It won't help anyone if you overheat and blow a gasket."
Charlotte

~⑤~

Daring to Dream
What a victory!

You'll feel a real sense of accomplishment when you hear "Pomp and Circumstance" and see the turning of tassels at high school graduation. But you can't sit back and relax yet. A lot of decisions must be made as your teen prepares to leave home.

Plan to shift gears as your child comes to the fork in the road. Confusion abounds as your student faces so many important life choices. You know your graduate is thinking: "Which way should I go? College? Take a year off and work? Get married? Join the military?"

Be prepared. Your young adult may not follow your road map. Remember, there's more than one way to get from Point A to Point B. Sometimes your teen needs to take a detour to know what works.

Many of our children have changed directions. They've done the tour of colleges from SMU to Texas Tech with a few stops along the way. After starting out wanting to be doctors or lawyers, they were sucked into beer pong and drafted into beverage management. And then, once on the interview circuit, they decided to exchange their power suits for bathing suits while sorting out their next stops.

Talk about trying—or should that be crying?—times. A routine meeting with your friends can be great therapy. In our weekly sessions, we've learned to do the following:

Let go—You have to give your young adults room for trial and error.

Dare to dream—But don't force *your* dreams on them.

Bite your tongue—Keep your opinions to yourself.

Be positive—Your confidence can empower them.

Hang in there—Some paths have more curves (maybe even U-turns) than others.

Give hugs—No matter what their age, they'll always be your babies.

You've done your best to equip them for their travels. Now, let them move into the driver's seat.

—e

*"Encouragement can have more impact than
I-told-you-sos." Shelley*

—e

"Are We There Yet?"
It's not the destination; it's the journey. This road trip called life has brought our families closer.

What has held us together through the twists and turns and kept us from going over a cliff? A glance in the rearview mirror reveals our girlfriends made the difference. With time, the village grew and merged to include our husbands and eighteen children. That made our trip easier and more enjoyable and had a huge impact on our kids. Besides having their parents to keep them accountable, they also had an extended family of friends.

Our children have the love and support of eight families. We were there for the activities and milestones: soccer games, dance recitals, concerts, football games, birthday parties, graduations, and marriages.

We were there when Cole's band debuted at *The Door* in Fort Worth. As a teenager, Charlotte's son was the lead singer in a Christian rock group called *Where's My Latte?* Wanting to make an evening of it, we grabbed our husbands, had dinner, and drove to the concert.

Talk about a generation gap! We were the seniors in the crowd that night. Although we tried to look hip, the music blared so loud we could hardly hear, let alone understand, the words. A few minutes in, Bob, Cole's dad, disappeared. When he returned wearing earplugs, we couldn't help but laugh while asking, "Where're ours?" We still tease him about that.

We might have sacrificed our hearing, but it was all worth it when, after the set, Cole joined his groupies in the audience and said our show of support rocked his night.

Cole, Charlotte, and Terri several years later after our budding musician's band had been renamed Verae.

This experience demonstrates the value of our village. Although our eighteen kids aren't all best friends (some are closer than others), they're bonded for life. Whenever we're lucky enough to get everyone together, they enjoy catching up on the here and now and reminiscing about the past.

Another testimony is that all our children say, "We want what you have...friends that become your family." That tells us we've arrived!

⟶⟶

"Talk about a generation gap. As we age, it feels more like a great divide!" Debbie

⟶⟶

4
Outrunning Age

Thong-a-Tude
The unseen can empower you, instantly making you feel ten years younger and ten pounds thinner.

When you hear old age knocking at your door, lace up your Nikes and run. Or walk. Or bike. Or swim...anything to keep you from falling into a lethargic limbo. Don't give in to flab, cellulite, low energy, or aching joints without a fight. Quit making excuses and get started.

Set Realistic Goals
Take a long look in the mirror. If you're anything like us, you zero in on any areas needing improvement. We struggle with

back fat, muffin tops, thunder thighs, and countless other issues depending on who you ask. Sound familiar?

Unfortunately, no miracle cures exist. Believe us…we've searched high and low. You may never be a size 0 like Charlotte. (Who else could survive on a steady diet of pickles and graham crackers as she did for years? It's just not possible, let alone healthy.) But don't be discouraged. With a little determination, anyone can make a change.

Are you up for an upgrade? Ready or not, here we go:

Take stock—Start by asking "How can I be a happier, healthier me?" Make a list with two columns: things you like about yourself and things you want to change. Be positive and realistic. Shelley likes her long, lean legs but wants to lift and tone her booty. Becky has pretty shoulders but thinks she needs to work on her jiggly arms. Bev has amazing abs but would be thrilled with thinner thighs.

Chart your course—What motivates you? Are you a self-starter or do you need help? Whether you're a competitive go-getter or an expert procrastinator, you can map out a health-and-fitness plan that works. After surviving breast cancer, Charlotte insisted on doing everything possible to prevent recurrence. Exercise and nutrition became a top priority. She decided to make Wii Fit her workout buddy, charge forward with a low-fat diet, and amp up the veggies at each meal.

Get off your rear—Stop making excuses and just do it. The threat of osteoporosis and a desire to look and feel younger got Linda moving. Her job keeps her sitting at a desk all day, so she made a new year's resolution to exercise more. Since her StairMaster had become an extension of her closet, she joined a health club and was soon working out regularly. Now she feels better and has energy to spare.

Journal your journey—Do you ever wonder why the scale seems stuck? Start jotting down your habits. Recording when, what, and how much you eat along with how you feel can reveal the good, the bad, and the ugly. Debbie did just that when she became discouraged a month after joining yoga and water aerobics classes. What was wreaking havoc on her diet? A hard look at her daily routine quickly showed it was her addiction to Chick-fil-A's chicken biscuits in the a.m. and McAlister's sweet tea in the p.m.

If you want to see change, make a plan and challenge yourself. You don't have to run a marathon, but you *can* walk around the block. Bottom line, everyone is different. Accept your individuality, and find what works for you.

"When you hear old age knocking at your door, lace up your Nikes and run!" Linda

Commit to Healthy Habits

We can't change some things about ourselves. We're stuck with our height, bone structure, and basic body build (unless we resort to extreme plastic surgery!). But we can stop supersizing at Sonic and tackle the treadmill to lay the groundwork for healthier, happier habits.

For a life-lift, we recommend eating right, exercising consistently, and eliminating excesses.

Eat Clean

Here's our recipe for healthy eating:

Plan your meals—It may take time, but think ahead. Check a website like EatingWell.com for simple, nutritious menus and a ready shopping list. Then don't stray. Otherwise, you risk giving in to temptations such as Oreos, Shiner Bock, and Blue Bell. That's especially true if you shop on an empty stomach or with a man!

Nix processed foods—You can do this by shopping the outer edges of the grocery store for fresh fruits, vegetables, dairy products, and meats. Stay far away from the cookie, cracker, and cereal aisles. Instead of giving in to Cocoa Puffs, get your crunch from carrot sticks, cucumbers, or other raw veggies.

Limit anything white—This includes sugar, flour, pasta, rice, breads, potatoes, and most starches. Go for a rainbow, filling your plate and your palate with whole grains, leafy vegetables, and colorful fruits. Afraid you'll miss your comfort foods? Just remember, nothing tastes as good as healthy feels.

⎯⎯⎯⌇⎯⎯⎯

"Say no to whites so you can say yes to the little black dress." Becky

⎯⎯⎯⌇⎯⎯⎯

Count your calories—Every little nibble adds up. A Cinnabon may seem heavenly, but eat just one, and you've probably used more than half your daily calorie quota. Need help? Try an app like Calorie Counter by MyFitnessPal or the MyPlate Calorie Tracker by Livestrong.com to keep a running tab.

Raise your glass—We're talkin' H_2O...sorry, wine and Diet Coke don't count! Water's benefits are endless. This miracle worker refreshes, cleanses, and purifies. Water also provides a natural way to help your skin look younger, cure headaches, and prevent muscle cramps. So here's to toasting hydration. Bottom's up!

Lean on protein—Bored with beef, chicken, and fish? Think greek yogurt, hummus, almonds, black beans, or lentils. Eating four to six ounces of protein at mealtime is healthy, satisfying, and can help you get better results from your workout.

How to Dine Out Without Pigging Out

Start with a dressing drink.

Make a fruittini (sixteen ounces of water with an assortment of fresh fruit). It's our favorite for taking a bite out of your appetite. Think sangria with water in place of wine.

Skip calorie-packed appetizers.

- Nix the chips and bread.
- Bring on the raw veggies, a simple green salad, or a broth-based soup. (Sorry, no lobster bisque!)

Practice portion control.

- Get a to-go box at the start of the meal and put half your food in it.
- Order lunch portions at dinner or select from the kids menu.
- Share meals. Waiters hate us, but we split everything.
- Think thin thighs instead of supersizing.
- Ignore mom's clean-plate advice. Always leave something uneaten.

Cut calories where you can.

- Ditch the coffee cake and keep your lattes skinny.
- Scratch sautéed and fried foods; opt for grilled, broiled, or baked.
- Forget fries. Ask for a naked baked potato, steamed veggies, or fresh fruit.
- Don't graze. Fill your plate and back away from the buffet.
- Slow down. Put the brakes on your fast food habit.

Curb your condiments.

- Order salad dressing on the side (like in *When Harry Met Sally*). Better yet, use salsa.
- Just say no to sour cream, butter, and extra salt.
- Hold the mayo and try tangy mustard.
- Avoid gravies, sauces, and cream-based dishes.

Lighten up on dessert.

- Go for sherbet, sorbet, or low-fat frozen yogurt—not ice cream.
- Pick berries instead of cheesecake.
- Get your fix from heart-healthy dark chocolate.
- Order one dessert with several spoons—this is where girlfriends really come in handy.
- Break tradition. Order coffee without dessert or just have another fruittini!

Debbi, Shelley, Becky, Debbie, Bev, Linda, and Charlotte keep things light by ordering one dessert with seven spoons.

Exercise...A Lot

If you want an antiaging remedy, try exercise. It's never too late to start.

Put first things first—No excuses. You've got to move it to lose it, so make physical activity a priority. Charlotte always starts the day with a workout. She knows if she doesn't do it first thing, it won't get done. But Debbi finds it easier to exercise in the evening. After a busy day, she immediately heads for the walking trail to decompress.

Come equipped for results—Whatever your sport, having the right gear is more important than being stylish (although normally fashion rules). Take it from Becky who learned the hard way. Don't buy trendy running shoes from a pimply faced teenager filling in as summer help. Educate yourself, and take the time to be fitted properly by a seasoned shoe specialist.

Find a fitness friend—A partner keeps you accountable, encourages you, and makes the whole experience more fun. Terri invested in a health club membership but seldom darkened the door. That all changed when Debbie offered to share her personal trainer, and Terri began to see results. Of course, their plan worked better when they didn't stop at Krispy Kreme on the way home.

Shake up your routine—Are you bored with the treadmill? Try using an elliptical trainer, lifting weights, or attending aerobic classes. A little variety adds spice and improves your overall results. After years of strength training, Shelley decided to attempt the Leukemia & Lymphoma Society Team-in-Training marathon. She sweated for months, and we all cheered when she crossed the finish line. Not a bad way to celebrate turning forty!

*Debbi, Becky, Shelley, Debbie, and Charlotte take
a hike while visiting Lake Tahoe.*

Just keep moving—Get off the couch and walk the dog, play soccer with the kids, or wash your car. Even dancing to the radio while you dry your hair can burn calories. Bev needed a milder form of exercise after major surgery, so she dug into gardening. She was surprised at how many muscles she used bending, stretching, and lifting to plant. Now, besides being toned and tanned, she has a showstopping landscape.

*"Think outside the box. A fitness friend can be
four legged and furry." Debbi*

Eliminate Excesses

Sometimes it takes more than just healthy-eating habits and rigorous exercise to feel good about you. Often, we make the mistake of trying to fill the void by working eighty hours a week, shopping compulsively, or drinking six Diet Cokes a day. We've also been known to eat a whole box of Thin Mints in one sitting.

We all have weaknesses that can become bad habits whether they're the result of emotional baggage or just bad choices. Anything taken to excess can wreak havoc on your life and those around you. Look within and be totally honest.

Find out what is controlling you so you can work on controlling it. Start by identifying the problem, and then take ownership of the situation. Picture your life free of addictions and think about all you'll gain: time, money, better health, and stronger relationships to name a few. Adopt a new attitude and begin eliminating excesses one day at a time.

Change begins with you but you don't have to go it alone. Appoint a girlfriend as your CPA (certified personal advisor) to help audit your lifestyle and create a healthy balance. You can count on girlfriends for honesty and support.

⤳

"You know it's an addiction when you plan your day around Sonic's happy hour." Linda

⤳

Get a Reality Checkup

Eating right and exercising are just the first steps toward a healthy lifestyle. As women, we typically put ourselves on the back burner. We're so busy juggling family and career demands that we don't take care of ourselves. We postpone mammograms to go to parent-teacher conferences, cancel pap smears to nurse sick children, and miss dental appointments because of work deadlines.

You should take charge of your own health care—and that means preventive maintenance. Keep doctor appointments like you keep hair appointments. Instead of ignoring yourself, do your research and check off your checkups:

- Know your family medical history.
- Monitor suspicious moles and skin rashes.
- Watch for changes in your sleeping or eating habits.
- Conduct monthly breast self-exams.
- Have a physical and see your gynecologist annually.
- Schedule mammograms, colonoscopies, and bone density tests as recommended by your doctor.
- Undergo stress tests to check your heart health.
- Maintain dental hygiene with biannual cleanings.

Stop making excuses, look for warning signs, and listen to your body. It's up to *you* to take care of *you.*

*"Set checkup reminders on your smartphone. Be
proactive now so you can stay active later." Shelley*

Reward Yourself

Aah—success can be as sweet as double-fudge chocolate
brownies. It fills you with satisfaction, brings a smile to your
face, and makes you desire more. When you see yourself reaching your dream, go ahead, indulge and reward yourself—you
deserve it!

Charlotte's reward is on a daily basis. She cuts out breakfast, eats
a teeny-tiny lunch, and treats herself to a normal dinner with
dessert. This routine keeps her weight down, so she never feels
deprived.

Shelley rewards herself weekly. Her rigorous boot camp-style
exercise routine begins at 5:30 a.m. Monday through Friday.
She gives herself a break by sleeping late and relaxing on
Saturday and going to church on Sunday. By taking the week-
end off, she's rejuvenated and ready to start working out again
Monday.

Debbie rewards herself at the end of each month. She maintains a walking regime and checks off each day on her calendar. She visualizes her accomplishment, and then comes her reward—a massage. This calming quiet time relieves her stress and leaves her feeling refreshed.

Linda, Becky, Shelley, and Bev are always happy to join Debbie (far right) when she rewards herself with a massage at a Dallas spa.

Here are some ways you might reward yourself:

- Go to Barnes and Noble and sip Starbucks while you browse.
- Take a long soak in the tub with your favorite mindless entertainment magazine.
- Walk through furniture stores to get decorating ideas.
- See a chick flick by yourself, so you don't have to share the popcorn.

- Ooh and aah over designer shoes or jewelry you can't afford.
- Splurge on a Godiva chocolate-covered strawberry.
- Stroll through an outdoor market on a beautiful sunny day.
- Sneak off for a weekend getaway at a bed-and-breakfast.

In writing this book, we rewarded ourselves along the way. As we completed each chapter, we celebrated with a champagne toast. Take time to acknowledge your victories, and you'll be encouraged and motivated to continue.

"Create your own personal reward card redeemable for whatever warms your heart and makes you smile." Terri.

5
Creating a Fabulous You

Thong-a-Tude
A flirty thong can be your little beauty secret. This pretty foundation lifts your mood and makes you feel booty-licious. Shhhh...no one needs to know but you.

Are you stuck in a time warp?

Has CoverGirl been your go-to gal from puberty to menopause? Are you sporting the same hair style pictured in your high school yearbook? Do the fashion police have a warrant out for your arrest?

If you're guilty of any of these, you're not alone—we've all been there. We shudder to think what we'd be like today without our girlfriends. Becky would be smackin' Dr. Pepper-flavored lip gloss, Bev would still have long feathered Farrah hair, and Debbi would be wearing gaudy Christmas sweaters. Girlfriends can keep you fashionable and fun.

Get ready to expand your horizons, trade in your granny panties, and break through to a fabulous you.

Being Hip, Not Hoochie

OK, girls. We all want to look younger, but beware of crossing the fine line between hip and hoochie.

You might be a hoochie if

- you're over thirty and wearing daisy dukes with your UGGs;
- your bling is in your belly button instead of on your finger;
- your jeans ride so low your thong shows;
- the girls are busting out of your bustier;
- your bleached hair looks brassy, not classy.

You don't have to dress like a teen to get the "in" look.

Being hip means following the trends and adapting them to your individual style. Even if you have an awesome body, you cross the line when you don't consider your age. Avoid clothes that are too tight, too revealing, or too skanky. Instead, focus on updating your makeup, clothing, and hair.

$$\backsim$$

"You can't be forever twenty-one but you can look fabulous at fifty." Debbie

$$\backsim$$

Makeup Is a Must

Makeup can work miracles, evening out your skin tone, hiding imperfections, and brightening your eyes and lips. But if you're caking on sparkly blue eye shadow and heavy lip liner with no thought of blending, run—don't walk—to your nearest department store cosmetic counter where you can find (almost) free help.

One of the best times to take advantage of a free makeover is when you hear time ticking as you approach a zero year. We call these years "makeover milestones" because they're the perfect opportunity to freshen up our looks.

Age Thirty: The Mommy Makeover

As we say good-bye to our twenties, many women struggle with the demands of career and family. A shortage of sleep, a lack of me time, and whacked-out hormones can take a real toll on a youthful glow.

When our Noxzema-girl Debbi turned thirty, her skin started screaming for attention—much like her three preschoolers. With her free-gift offer in hand, she called Linda and suggested they go for a complimentary makeover at the mall. The Clinique expert gave them a real education on skin care products, helping them avoid cosmetics confusion. Debbi found a moisturizer perfect for her changing skin and saw how a quick touch of mascara and lip gloss could really perk up her look.

A busy mom of three, our Noxzema-girl Debbi takes a break with Charlotte and Charlotte's son, Cole.

Like many young moms, Debbi had been tempted to go au naturel until she discovered makeup-on-the-go. She started getting up a few minutes earlier to follow these simple steps:

- Use a touch of concealer to hide undereye circles.
- Apply mascara to brighten the eyes.

- Dust the cheeks with a blush of color.
- Add a hint of shine with lip gloss.

Even the busiest mom can find a few minutes for this easy mini-makeover. You'll be surprised how much it can improve your look and attitude.

Beauty Tip for Your Thirties

Keep it simple. You're so busy wiping bottoms and noses that you don't have time to wipe tons of makeup off your face.

Age Forty: The Midlife Makeover

Lights, camera, action...forty sets the stage for an eye-enhancing experience. The many roles we play take a heavy toll on our appearance as well as our emotions. Bleary eyes and dark circles appear as natural side effects to dealing with teenagers, who can't help but be challenging. (You just *thought* you didn't get sleep in your thirties...at least you knew where your children *were*.)

If plastic surgery isn't an option, just find your inner makeup artist. You're in luck if you have daughters—or better yet, girl-friends—because they are all too happy to help.

Terri has no reason to visit the makeup counter. Her beautiful daughters, Stephanie, Allison, Kelli, and Ashley, know all the latest techniques. One evening on the way out to a black-tie gala, Terri and her husband, Mike, stopped to have the girls snap a pic.

"Hey, Mom, let us accent your eyes," Allison offered.

The girls whisked Terri to the bathroom, and a few minutes later, she emerged looking ready for the red carpet. She learned how to play up her eyes by

- darkening her eyebrows to frame her face;
- applying smoky eye shadow for evening;
- using black eye liner to make her eyes pop;
- finishing the look with a double dose of lash-lengthening mascara.

Whether you're on the runway or the freeway, remember, your eyes are the window to your soul. Let them shine.

Beauty Tip for Your Forties

Invest in your eyes. Stock up on antiaging serums, moisturizing creams and drops, and eye-enhancing makeup. You may be forty, but your eyes won't give you away!

Age Fifty: The Menopausal Makeover

In our twenties, we thought we looked hot. But in our fifties, we *are* hot. We have entered what we fondly call "hormonal hell." (This *is not* the kind of tropical vacation we had in mind!)

We blame changing "hor-moans" for all our misery and wretchedness: age spots, thinning and feathery lips, facial hair, and deepening lines. Plus, everything is beginning to dry up…and we mean *everything*. We are all looking for our own fountain of youth!

But no worries...this is where girlfriends and antiaging products come in handy.

> *Like most of us, Linda is on a constant quest to defy age. When Lancôme's new collagen treatment came out, she made a beeline to Dillard's on her lunch hour. To her dismay, the shelves were bare—the product she had to have was sold out. Desperation set in! Needing instant gratification as well as a facial fix, she kept searching. Three stores later, she found the coveted collagen and purchased it without even questioning the cost.*

> *She snuck back to the office, heels in hand, and got right on her computer to start spreading the news about her find. While on her high-tech beauty hotline, she learned about a new lip plumper and began planning her next makeup mission.*

Linda's endless search for the best has helped us weed out the good, the bad, and the overhyped. We've learned

- it helps to have someone else do the research. (If you don't have a friend like Linda, you can always pick up *InStyle* magazine for the latest and greatest beauty tips.);
- you can't expect cover girl results. No matter how much lip plumper you buy, you'll never look like Angelina Jolie;
- the most expensive products are not necessarily the best. Experiment with everything from L'Oréal to La Mer.

Look at turning fifty as an adventure…a new beginning. Remember, fifty is the new thirty. Be courageous and don't give up the quest. Hope is as close as the nearest cosmetics counter.

Beauty Tip for Your Fifties

Hydrate, lubricate, and when all else fails…fabricate!

Age Sixty: The Mature versus Matronly Makeover
If fifty is the new thirty, sixty *must* be the new forty. At least, that's our prayer. We're not all sixty yet, so we'll make this section short and sweet!

As Dolly Parton's character Truvy says in *Steel Magnolias*, "Honey, time marches on and eventually you realize it is marchin' across your face." There comes an age (and sixty might be it) where you have to accept the pull of gravity and be comfortable in your own skin. We hope to handle the inevitable with grace and style but a little fudging never hurts. Surgical enhancements are becoming so refined and affordable you can fit them in between the gym and grandkids.

Wear your age with confidence! You can still be sassy and sexy at sixty.

You are beautiful at every stage, and it helps to have girlfriends to remind you.

Beauty Tip for Your Sixties

Girlfriends can be your fountain of youth. They help you think fashionable, not frumpy; sassy, not sloppy; modern, not matronly.

Hair Is Huge

What's a cake without icing, a package without a bow, a margarita without salt? B-o-r-i-n-g! The same could be said for anyone without the right hairstyle. Even Sarah Jessica Parker in her Manolo Blahnik stilettos, Dolce & Gabbana sequin gown, Harry Winston jewels, Judith Leiber crystal bag, and expertly applied Chanel makeup can't walk the red carpet with Marge Simpson hair.

Your hair is your crowning glory, your signature. In addition to topping off your look, it dictates your mood. We have a hard time feeling good if our hair doesn't work. That's why to us, and to all women, hair is *h-u-g-e*.

Of all the topics in this book, nothing stirred up as much emotion as our hair. Everything is bigger in Texas…especially hair. As Texans, our hair and hair issues seem larger than life. We're passionate about hair—what's wrong with it and how we can fix it.

Splitting Hairs

Our girlfriend group has a lot that binds us together, but hair creates a great divide. On one side, we have the flat-and-fine (Becky and Charlotte); on the other, the full-and-frizzy (Linda, Debbie, Terri, and Debbi); and caught in between, the fabulous few (Bev and Shelley), those darn lucky girls with the perfect hair.

We start splitting hairs as soon as we hear the hair weather forecast. When Al Roker predicts rain, Becky fears her style will fall along with the barometric pressure. She packs a teasing comb, heavy-duty volumizer, and ponytail holder as a last resort. Meanwhile, the same forecast causes Linda to panic over the possibility of really big hair. She won't leave home without her rainy-day survival kit: antifrizz serum and Control Freak hairspray.

Although Becky and Linda turn to different products, they experience similar feelings. To both girls, rain clouds signal a red alert: *warning, warning...bad hair day ahead!*

This sets the tone for their whole day. Who wouldn't be tempted to call in sick at the thought of under-the-weather hair? It's like a huge zit on your nose. You can't face the world with confidence when you know people are staring at your crappy coiffure.

Girls, we've all encountered this at one time or another. Instead of suffering in silence, talk to your friends. Chances are they've been there. Knowing you're not alone can make it easier to weather Mother Nature's wrath.

Hair Emergency Preparedness Kit

Every girl needs a hair emergency kit in her purse, her car, her desk, or all three that includes the following:

A battery-operated curling iron—Perfect for prepresentation touchups.

Pomade—Just a pinch gives you a sleek, smooth, shiny finish.

A purse-size pick—It provides a quick, late-afternoon lift.

Hairspray—Nothing works for thick hair like Sebastian.

A butterfly clip—Pulling your hair up in a half ponytail is an instant facelift.

A trendy headband—It's the little black dress of hair accessories.

Making the Cut

What do you want your hair to say when you walk into a room? Dark roots and split ends scream your hurried lifestyle leaves no time for the salon. A Dorothy Hamill wedge says you're stuck in the eighties and afraid to move ahead. Streaks of gray are a sure sign you've gone from the mommy track to the granny track.

If this isn't the impression you want to leave, think about a change. Look for new ideas. People watch, check out fashion magazines, and Google what's trending. Ask for help from your friends and family in addition to your hair stylist. Be prepared for honest answers. Don't just sit there—take action, like our friend Harriet did in her "Hair Affair to Remember." Of course, we've changed her name to protect the innocent.

> *Overnight, Harriet decided her long, straight strands really dated her. They just hung there, kind of like grandma's drapes. She went on a hunt for a fresh, contemporary style. Harriet became a hair stalker, walking the malls looking for a dramatic new do. When she finally found it, she boldly approached the stranger and said, "I love your hair. Who cuts it?"*
>
> *"Oh, that would be Kaitlin," the woman answered. "She's the best."*
>
> *Thus began Harriet's hair affair. She quickly called Kaitlin to make an appointment, and then drove miles to hide her indiscretion. She told herself no one would get hurt; it was just this once, and then she'd return to Sandra, her long-time stylist. At the salon, Harriet described the subject of her hair envy, and Kaitlin said, "Ah, yes. It will be a new you."*

Fifty shades of fabulous later, Harriet left, feeling totally satisfied.

Trying to do the right thing, she decided to stay close to home for her next cut. She hoped Sandra could recreate the experience she had with Kaitlin. But Sandra wasn't up to the challenge. She could no longer meet Harriet's needs.

Realizing it was time to move on, Harriet tried Jeff, then Tiffany, and eventually went back to Kaitlin. She'd officially become a hair whore.

Harriet's quest for a new style helped her realize that change could look and feel good. If your hair isn't making the cut, follow Harriet's example:

Embrace change—Don't get locked in to one style.

Be observant—Look for new ideas on Pinterest and Instagram as well as in magazines, malls, and the media.

Be complimentary—When you see a style you love, ask "Who does your hair?"

Be willing to break up—Both you and your longtime hairdresser may be in a rut.

If you're lucky enough to have that rare hair stylist who recommends new looks, hang on to her. If not, don't hesitate to try someone new. A change could be just what you need.

—❧—

"Be willing to break up with your longtime hair-dresser. You both may be in a rut." Charlotte

—❧—

Products, Procedures, and Paraphernalia

Now that you have the perfect cut, how do you keep looking like you just stepped out of the salon? You can't do it alone. You need a bag full of tricks to help manage your mop.

Do your products fit in a tote or a trunk? During a recent round-table discussion, we revealed all our dirty hair secrets and discovered we're chemically dependent! We fear withdrawal and the certain highs and lows if we don't have our daily fix. We all need volumizers, mousse, gels, and hair serums just to make it through the day. And don't even get us started on our must-have tools. Our inventory includes everything from one dollar clippies to one hundred dollar Chi ceramic flatirons.

However, some of us have more *baggage* than others. Hence, the great divide between the full-and-frizzy, the flat-and-fine, and the fabulous few.

Taming the Beast

The full-and-frizzies argue their hair is the most challenging. Like a toddler, it's time-consuming, rebellious, and demanding. Each day begins with a battle. You fight to style your unruly mane, walk outside, and immediately lose control.

Debbie's struggled with her hair for years. Her intensive program takes her into a zone of her own. *No one* does their do like Debbie does. Talk about a workout.

> *Debbie's elaborate hair-a-thon rules her life. She plans her week around the lengthy ordeal. Step one begins the night before with a Kérastase hot-oil treatment. The next morning, she uses hydrating shampoo and conditioner before combing her hair out in the shower. While it air dries, Debbie grabs a water and protein bar, slips into athletic shoes, and prepares herself for the big hair workout to come. She warms up by throwing her head over and massaging an oil-and-gel cocktail from the roots to the tips of her thick locks.*

> *To get ready for her power set, she reaches for her indispensable Chi tools: flatiron, blow-dryer, and round, ceramic brush. She depends on them so much she's become emotionally attached.*

> *At this point, timing is everything. Debbie hangs a do-not-disturb sign on her door and ignores the phone because any interruption could mean the dreaded do-over. Dividing her*

hair into three sections, she begins the drying process, which turns into a forty-five-minute upper body routine.

Afterward, Debbie sprays her hair with Kenra and pulls it into a half ponytail. She does her makeup and folds a load of clothes, taking a breather before entering the next phase. Flatiron in hand, she loosens her locks, smooths the top layers, and applies pomade to define the look. With what little energy she has left, Debbie goes for a final dose of hairspray, and then she's out the door—a mere three hours after the process began.

Debbie may be exhausted from her hair Olympics, but one glance in the mirror gives her a second wind. Just ask her husband, Jerry. She has a gold-medal look that frees her from fretting over her frizzies for three "un-hair-ied" days.

Pump Up the Volume

The flat-and-fine need a little extra TLC to pump up the volume. Their daily, sometimes twice daily, process is just as time-consuming as the full-and-frizzies'. The whole routine has to be choreographed, and the moves must have perfect timing.

Becky's hair ordeal has rhythm, but she's still singin' the blues. Although she starts on a high-hair note, it often falls flat by day's end. Every morning, Becky heads straight to the shower to shampoo and condition.

With the clock ticking, she doesn't want to wake her sleeping husband, Jay...no time for romance. She moves quickly to the hall bath where she tangos with her tangles before pumping up the volume. She pulls out the big guns for the big blowout: Aquage Uplifting Foam, Aveda Root Stimulator, and a high-powdered hair dryer.

The tempo quickens. She blow-dries and then Velcro rolls it, spritzing some spray along the way. She hustles back to the other bathroom for a touchup with the curling iron and a little tease. Then she's ready to rock and roll.

For one special moment, Becky looks like the belle of the ball as she waltzes out the door. Too bad her flattering do is fleeting. For tomorrow, the dance begins again.

"Flat-and-fine hair has no memory. You have to reteach it every day." Becky

Blow 'n Go

Compared to their friends' rigorous routines, the fabulous few find hair care a walk in the park. Their fifteen-minute prep arouses hair envy in the rest of the group because these low-maintenance girls scoot out the door in no time.

Remember Bev, our natural blond? We have a love-hate relationship with her. We love her and her hair, but we hate how easy she has it. Her balding husband, Tommy, spends more time on his hair than she does.

Bev's worry-free process is a dream. With four short steps, hair care is no chore. Wash, blow-dry, curl, and spray, and she's out the door. She swears by Sebastian Volupt products, any generic hairspray, and a weekly, deep-cleansing shampoo like Neutrogena.

Bigger occasions call for bigger hair, so Bev adds Velcro rollers for special events. They give her hair the extra boost it needs to get that authentic Dallas diva look.

Whether she's off to the park or to a party, Bev's fix-and-forget-it hair remains a fantasy for the rest of us. We long to be part of the fabulous few...but it's an exclusive club.

Hair can ruin your day or rock your world. Accept the power your hair holds over you, and deal with it.

Bev and Linda caught before and after their styling routines.

Whether you're full-and-frizzy, flat-and-fine, or one of the fabulous few,

Hair Is Huge!

Big hair, flat hair, curly or straight;
Hair's *huge* with women, there's no debate.

With so many products from which to choose
Why not try them all—what do I have to lose?

Will I need mousse, volumizer, straightener, or gel?
Freeze, goop, mud, detangler? Oh, hell!

What have I done? Now, it's plastered to my head.
My hair won't move. It looks lifeless and dead.

So many challenging issues to face
The daily hair forecast takes first place.

Will my hair frizz? Will it flop?
Will I need a wig? No, maybe a mop!

Sun, rain, wind, and humidity determine the course.
Tools and products help fight the battle with force.

Oh, the hours spent drying and styling my hair.
Gosh, I'm late for work…but I don't care.

I'm so frustrated I wanna shave my head,
Give up, call in sick, and go back to bed.

Yes, hair is huge—number one on my list.
A new style, color, and cut I cannot resist.

I'll never surrender to the slightest touch of gray—
Highlighting and coloring to keep it away.

All this worry, time, and expense is making me *mad*
'Cause I *still* don't look like the magazine ads.

It's exhausting, but I'll never give in.
I'll keep on fightin' until the bitter end.

At my final hour, with my loved ones there,
One last request…please fix my hair!

I want to meet my Maker for that grand date
Looking my very best as I enter Heaven's gate!

Fashion Adds Flair

Your makeup looks great, and for the moment, your hair is perfect. How do you select clothes to complete your look? You're at a crossroads. Will you make a fashion faux pas or finish with finesse?

Check yourself out. Are you guilty of any of the following style stoppers?

Wearing clothes that date you—Ill-fitting mom jeans accentuate your butt and gut.

Choosing the wrong size—Going too-small reveals every ripple while oversized pieces conceal every curve.

Raiding your daughter's closet—*Just because you can...*doesn't mean you should.

Providing visual overstimulation—Too much of a good thing quickly becomes overkill.

Showing your panty lines—The ultimate no-no shouts, "I'm proud of my panties."

If so, let us rescue you from what could be a fatal fashion fiasco. We've all committed crimes of fashion, pled guilty, and served our time. You can learn from our mistakes.

Boost Your Bounty

No matter what your shape, you can do things to enhance it. Take our friend little Debbi.

She has been on a mission to find a natural-looking padded bra since puberty. In desperation, she's tried everything:

- *White tube socks, borrowed from her brother, were uneven and lumpy*

- *Wonder bra proved to be not so wonderful when she had nothing to work with*
- *Water bra was incredibly heavy, and she always feared springing a leak.*

Eventually, little Debbi sought some professional help from a Nordstrom lingerie specialist. She put aside her inhibitions, and let Rosie bring out the tape measure for a personalized fitting.

"I've got just the thing," Rosie offered. "Wacoal makes a petite padded bra that'll fit you perfectly."

"Really!? A petite bra?" Debbi exclaimed. "How'd I miss that?"

Minutes later, she was wearing a sexy black number that played up her figure naturally.

"Finally," she thought. "So long, pancakes. H-e-l-l-o, cupcakes!"

Finding something that felt customized made all the difference. Whether you're a flat-chested Debbi or a voluptuous Vivian, the proper fit can keep the girls in line: no more *hiding out or hanging out in all the wrong places.*

Now, turn around and check your rear view in the mirror. Could you be picked out of a panty lineup? A proper fit is just as important for your booty as it is for your boobies. Your backside can reveal your most intimate secrets.

You can't conceal the evidence without help from a new friend. A skimpy little thong can eliminate all "telltail" signs of your bare necessities. Now, we know what you're thinking: "I'm too old. I'm overweight. I'm out of shape." And then, of course, "I'm a *nice* girl." But don't be afraid to try one. A thong can set you free. Once you get used to it, a thong feels very natural.

But beware—you may even forget you're wearing one like our girlfriend did on a flight home from a weekend getaway.

> *She'd dressed comfortably with a lacy red thong under her casual denim skirt, her favorite outfit for flying. Two Diet Cokes later, she made a mad dash for the airplane lavatory.*
>
> *Quickly locking the door, she lifted her skirt and squatted. Too late, she realized her thong was still in place! She removed it in a panic and flushed her eighteen-dollar splurge down the toilet. What else was a girl to do?*
>
> *Though she longed to stay put, she gathered her courage, smoothed her skirt, and walked back to her seat panty-less... Britney-style.*

You might never feel this comfortable, but a thong can become your second skin. Besides taking care of one of the biggest fashion faux pas (panty lines), a thong puts a swing in your step. It's a little secret that gives your confidence a big boost.

Although our top pick for that sexy, flirty feeling is a thong, sometimes we need a little more support to control rolls and ripples. Then Spanx can be your undercover, smooth-all-over solution, perfect for the clingiest fashions. Invented for women by a woman, this modern-day girdle can replace your panties or thong.

What's underneath is just as important as what people see. With the right little nothings, you're well on your way to achieving fashion finesse.

⸺ᗋ

"What's underneath can launch your look and give your attitude an edge." Terri

⸺ᗋ

Dress without Stress

When you step into your closet, is it like a scene from *A Nightmare on Elm Street*? Are you haunted by fashions from your past? Are you hanging onto skeletons from the 70s, 80s, and 90s? Do you have sizes ranging from two to ten covered with cobwebs?

Well, no wonder you're spooked. Who could get dressed with a closet screaming for help? Face your fears and purge your possessions. If doing it by yourself makes you squeamish, call your friends.

Our friend Terri has closet issues. We didn't realize how bad they were until Bev came to pick her up for one of our girlfriend weekends. Bev found Terri in a frantic frenzy, still in her robe, minutes before they were to be at a surprise brunch for Charlotte's fiftieth birthday.

Terri pointed to her empty suitcase and wailed "I haven't packed a thing!"

On the verge of tears, Terri anxiously dressed while rattling off what she wanted packed. Bev sprang into action, hunting for a weekend wardrobe. She climbed over boxes, a laundry basket, and holiday decorations that were blocking the door, entering the closet on a mission to find navy-blue pumps. Before her stood a literal mountain of shoes…this was not going to be easy. You have to know Terri. When she finds something that works, she buys it in several colors. The pumps obviously worked.

Finding a matching pair turned into a real scavenger hunt with the clock ticking. Bev grabbed shoes and jewelry to complement outfits Terri had laid out, stuffing everything into a bag. Terri glossed her lips, and out the door they ran.

That evening, as the eight of us dressed for a night on the town, Terri laughingly modeled one navy and one black pump. Thank goodness for dimly lit restaurants…no one else even noticed!

At Terri's insistence, we scheduled an emergency closet intervention shortly after we returned. You too can dress without stress if you: C-L-E-A-N U-P.

Clear the crap—your closet is for clothes. We started by clearing everything out of Terri's closet and sorting it into wearable and unwearable piles.

Lose the emotional attachment to sentimental favorites. We counseled Terri on getting rid of old prom dresses, Halloween costumes, and dried flower arrangements. Even she admitted she could've opened a vintage shop!

Employ help—professional or otherwise. If your budget allows, options range from hiring an organization expert to purchasing a closet system like those from California Closets or The Container Store. If not, turn to your friends. They usually work for free or for wine, like we did. Any excuse for a party!

Arrange like items and coordinate colors. We categorized Terri's clothes into casual, professional, and evening. Then we grouped jeans, slacks, sweaters, shirts, skirts, and dresses by season and color. We stored shoes in clear bins, hung belts on racks, and put purses on pegs.

Navigate between three bags: throwaway, giveaway, and store away. We quizzed Terri about each article, asking "Have you worn this in the last two years?" If the answer was no, then the item had to go. It took hours (and a lot of wine), but we finally stripped Terri of her years of closet confusion.

Use your space wisely and make things more accessible. We encouraged Terri to hang pants and skirts on layered hangers, stack folded sweaters on shelves, and keep a stepstool handy for hard-to-reach areas. Her closet even had enough space to install a third clothes rod for her off-season wardrobe. We put frequently worn items in the front, seldom-worn things in the back. We staged her closet, going from sleeveless to long-sleeved tops and from pants to skirts to dresses.

Pledge to stay organized. Now that you've ditched your closet hang-ups, make a long-term commitment to staying clutter free. You'll relapse into old habits if you're not careful. That's why we all took the "oath of organization," and you should too.

Oath of Organization

I promise whatever I take out to wear
    I will replace in its spot and not leave on a chair.

I promise to put shoes in their proper bin,
    So I will be able to find and wear them again.

I promise whenever I shop and splurge
    I will return home, weed out, and purge.

I promise to avoid putting crap on the floor.
    I will no longer hide clutter behind a closed door.

I promise to move costumes, decorations, and junk.
    I will store collectables in the attic, garage, or a trunk.

I promise that if my clothes get too tight
    I will give it two years and then give up the fight.

I promise that as the temperatures change,
    I will take stock of my wardrobe and then rearrange.

I promise not to cling to trends gone by.
    I will give to Goodwill and not blink an eye!

_____   _____

Signed   Date

"Clear the crap…your closet is for clothes." Bev

Steppin' Out in Style
What's your shoe style?

Bev   loves her boots in the colder months but slides into flip-flops as Texas heats up. This prairie girl finds comfort and romance in flowing skirts and couture cowboy boots.

Becky   favors fashionable flats that complement her long, leggy look. She collects patent, animal print, and brightly colored ballet slippers for both casual and dressy occasions.

Debbi   is drawn to down-under, cozy UGGs and classic Minnetonka mocs. These easy styles match her youthful look and sensible demeanor.

Debbie   chooses strappy kitten heels for a fun, sexy look and just enough height. When she enters a room, every eye turns. Funny how a little one-inch heel gives her such a big boost.

Linda   gravitates to chic stilettos that convey confidence and style. Her closet includes everything from basic black suede to lipstick-red patent. She brings Manhattan style to our suburban circle.

Shelley   fancies fun flip-flops. Relaxed yet classy, they fit her busy life. She shows off her perfect pedicures in styles ranging from simple Sanuk flats to over-the-top Swarovski-crystal platforms.

Terri   stockpiles classic heels in every color. Our timeless pump princess picks up every round-, square-, and pointy-toed feminine favorite that catches her eye. Her charming, yet comfortable, shoes reflect her easygoing personality.

Charlotte   admits she's addicted to MBT walking shoes, which her husband has fondly nicknamed "make your butt tighter." By day, you'll seldom find her in anything other than smart stacked heels. But after five, she laces up her MBTs for an effortless workout whether she's cooking, cleaning, or shopping.

Regardless of your style, shoes shouldn't be an afterthought. They may be the last thing you put on, but they should be the first thing you consider when choosing an outfit.

Charlotte is our own Imelda Marcos. When building her new home, she designed her closet to showcase her shoe collection complete with glass-front shelves, a tufted ottoman, and a crystal chandelier. All she needs now is a piano player or a little elevator music to complete the shoe-salon ambiance.

You might think Charlotte is a shoe snob, but no, she shops everywhere from Kohl's to Nordstrom in search of the elusive size 5½. She found Nordstrom, in particular, very accommodating while shopping during her birthday weekend.

Surrounded by all of us, her favorite personal shoppers, she searched for the perfect shoe for an evening at an exclusive Dallas nightclub.

Knowing availability could be an issue in Charlotte's size, Shelley told the salesman, "Just bring 'em all out."

In no time, a surprising sea of shoes appeared at Charlotte's feet. To her amazement, she had choices. She purchased three dangerously high-heeled pairs: black-patent peep toes, brown strappy sandals, and sexy red stilettos.

That evening, the new black shoes made their debut in a spectacular way. We finished dressing—looking sizzling hot—when coincidentally, the hotel fire alarm sounded. (Hmm, we must have been hotter than we thought!) We raced down three flights of stairs—although it felt like fifteen to Charlotte wearing those dangerously high heels. At the bottom, we found ourselves outside the W's trendy five-star restaurant—where we noticed that Dallas's elite continued eating, totally indifferent to the emergency situation. What were they thinking, or maybe, what were they drinking? Whatever it was, we needed some of that.

Forgoing dinner, we rushed to the once famous Ghostbar's VIP elevator. We felt like celebrities passing the crowd waiting behind the red velvet rope. Seconds later, we stepped into another world. We were hoping for a time machine back to our disco days but were launched into an ultra-modern techno scene. Charlotte immediately wondered if her shoes were up to the challenge.

Thanks to Charlotte's thoughtful husband, Bob, we were escorted to an incredible table overlooking the Ghostbar's renowned floating balcony. Stepping out of her comfort zone, Charlotte tentatively ventured onto the crystal-clear patio thirty floors above Dallas. She soon realized her mistake and shakily turned about-face, hurrying back inside.

Unfortunately her shoes had a mind of their own, and Charlotte toppled to the floor. Embarrassed, but without missing a beat, she quickly recovered and danced her way back to the table.

She had learned an important lesson. Shoes with dangerously high heels should come with a warning: "Wear with caution: best for standing, sitting, or display only."

Regardless, Charlotte was glad she'd stepped out and tried something different. No matter what your style, you need to have fun with your shoes. The right shoes can have a magical effect. They can even be life changing; just look what they did for Cinderella and Dorothy.

"Dare to walk on the wild side. A red stiletto can bring out the animal in you." Linda

Accessorize to Finalize

Annie may say, "You're never fully dressed without a smile," but we say, "You're never fully dressed without your bangles, earrings, necklaces, scarf, purse, and belt." Just to name a few of our favorite finishing touches.

Accessories complete your look like a frame completes a work of art. Simple, classy, or over the top, they make a statement, and reveal your personality. Everybody has a go-to little black dress—how you accessorize it sets the mood. Throw on a scarf and sunglasses for Saturday at the farmers' market. Add pearls and a jeweled clutch for an after-five wedding. Bring out your chunky turquoise bracelet and concho belt to switch things up for a patio party. The possibilities are endless.

Need help pulling it off? Just remember the following dos and don'ts:

Do   make your accessories accessible. Sort your jewelry by color, and keep it in a standing jewelry armoire or hanging organizer; then you can grab and go.

Do   use accessories for added pop. Mix them up instead of going all matchy-matchy. Avoid wearing the same color, pattern, or designer from head to toe.

Do   know when to stop. Accessories should attract, not distract, so practice self-control. We love layering necklaces and bracelets, pairing them with simple earrings. But choose wisely. More isn't always better. Sometimes it's just more.

Don't leave accessories to chance. Think ahead, have a plan, and bring your dress with you when shopping for finishing touches.

Don't supersize everything. You can get lost under a bulky scarf, enormous purse, and giant sunglasses. One big item increases your outfit's wow factor, but too many can overshadow it.

Don't think you have to spend a lot. Diamonds may be a girl's best friend, but costume jewelry is kinder to your wallet. Inexpensive trendy items can add zing without zapping your budget.

Linda, the queen of bling, has an eye for accessories. Addicted to everything from Target scarves to Tory Burch sunglasses, she's our AAA (accomplished accessory authority). We turn to her whenever an accessory crisis arises.

Debbie knew just who to call for help finalizing her elegant mother-of-the-bride ensemble. She started with a shimmering strapless bronze sheath complemented by an expensive silk wrap. In the store, the wrap fit perfectly, but once home, it wouldn't stay put. She had enough on her mind without worrying about a wardrobe malfunction.

She wrapped, wound, twisted, and tied, all to no avail. She even consulted a seamstress who refused to touch the fine delicate fabric because a mere pinprick could ruin it.

With the wedding days away, frustrated and at a loss for options, Debbie frantically called Linda. They met at Nordstrom, and within minutes, Linda had a solution to Debbie's dilemma—a jeweled hair clip, of all things. It secured the wrap beautifully, saving the day for Debbie. That little accessory provided the perfect finishing touch.

Be creative with accessories. They're a great opportunity to express your individuality. They can be the signature on the masterpiece: a fabulous new you!

⸺ࢣ⸺

"Choose accessories wisely. More isn't always better. Sometimes it's just more." Bev

⸺ࢣ⸺

Finding Your Thong-a-Tude
Congratulations!

You've got the look. You've got the style. Now, all you need to be red thong strong is a thong-a-tude: a liberating, empowering outlook that's gutsy, confident, and fun loving. It's time to shine and let things be about you. Don't wait a minute longer.

Here are our top ten ways to claim that thong-a-tude:

10. Face your fears…remember you're the boss.
9. Deal with today. Tomorrow's troubles will just make you gray.
8. Refresh your spirit: giving to others is a gift to yourself.
7. Get lost in a novel, in the mall, in a garden, in anything you enjoy.
6. Always keep learning. Smart is sexy at any age.
5. Take a hike…literally. Fresh air beats medication every time.
4. Laugh at yourself. It's a great, free antiaging treatment.
3. Accept your imperfections (easier done with complimentary lighting).
2. Become your dreams. Look at us: we wrote this book.

And the Number One way to claim a thong-a-tude is

Embrace the panty-free feeling. Indulge yourself: buy a flirty red thong and wear it proudly!

"Always keep learning. Smart is sexy at any age."
Becky

6
Exploring with Style

Thong-a-Tude
Travel light...leave your troubles and granny panties behind. You're sure to have more fun whether bound for a boutique or the beach.

Do you feel trapped in your daily routine? Is your mind so overloaded you drive off while still pumping gas? Are you so preoccupied you leave home and can't remember if you took your medicine, let the dog out, or shut the garage door?

Multitasking could be multistressing you. These are classic symptoms of what we like to call "restless life syndrome." What's the cure? We prescribe a strong dose of BFF time.

The best ways to relieve RLS involve time out with close friends. Shopping and travel work for us. For a quick fix, grab your cash, checkbook, and cards and head to the nearest retail hot spot. For longer-lasting relief, pack a bag and drive, cruise, or fly away for a mood-lifting holiday.

Prepping for Power Shopping

If your shopping life is less than satisfying, you aren't alone. Many women dread the unflattering fluorescent lights and unforgiving full-length mirrors. Waves of indecision, guilt, and frustration often accompany shopping for ourselves. That's why you need our three-step program, guaranteed to increase your shopping pleasure.

Step 1: Resolve

Lose the excuses. *You* are worth the time, money, and effort. Don't wait for a special occasion or anyone's approval. Grab a friend who can help you overcome your shopping hang-ups and live a little.

Resolve to make a day of it. Nothing can revive your attitude like a little retail therapy. To make the most of your time, use the following preshopping strategy:

Get a sitter—No kids allowed, whatever their age. Today is about you!

Do your hair and makeup—You'll feel better about yourself, and people will take notice.

Dress the part—Wear your best bra and undies. Choose a thong or no-line panties if you're shopping for skinny jeans, a pencil skirt, or anything clingy. Going nude (in color) always works.

Think quick-change artist—Easy on/off clothes are a must. Throw on a button-down shirt, a V neck top, or a sundress (you don't want to muss the diva do).

Add a cami underneath—Then you're set for trying on just about anything.

Slip on some stylish flats—That way you can look good while covering a lot of territory. Carry backup flip-flops for sole support later in the day.

Leave unnecessary jewelry at home—Why bring one more thing you have to think about in the dressing room?

Set your priorities—Lunch or shopping? Instead of losing time pigging out, pack a protein bar for that midday pick-me-up.

Be prepared—Bring a Texas-sized tote with mini hairspray, lipstick, comb, coupons, and your cell. Or cruise the cosmetic counters to freshen up.

Map out your strategy the day before—Fill up your tank, stop by the bank, and chart your course for shopping success.

Girlfriends Rule

Schedule retail therapy regularly just as you would your child's play dates.

Step 2: Tackle

Seize the day. Be willing to branch out by trying on anything and everything. If your closet is heavy on professional pieces, it might be time to add a sexy sundress. If black is your go-to color, shake things up with a pop of red, turquoise, or fuchsia.

Try not to fixate on size; it's just a number. If you love the look, but the hemline hits you wrong, the shoulders sag, or the waist is too big, consider alterations. A little nip and tuck can work wonders.

Don't tackle the decisions alone. If you're flying solo, ask a sales associate for help. Stores like Anthropologie, Nordstrom, and White House Black Market provide personal attention. Their stylists have an eye for the latest fashions and can help size up your wardrobe needs.

Remember, you want pieces that fit, flatter, and make you feel fabulous!

Girlfriends Rule

If you love the look but the fit's not quite right, ask about alterations. Stores such as Banana Republic and Nordstrom handle them free for cardholders.

Step 3: Succeed

Indulge yourself. You're always sensible, but now it's time to splurge, especially if you have a coupon.

Treat yourself to some sexy shoes, an edgy leather jacket, or a classy clutch. Making a decision will give you a real sense of accomplishment. Hang on to that shopping high as you triumphantly head to the next stop. As Yves Saint Laurent said, fashion is "not only to make women more beautiful, but also to reassure them, give them confidence."

As we approach fifty, we face a multitude of life changes. Talk about the sandwich generation—we're like a piece of Velveeta stuck between adult children and aging parents. Just like a grilled cheese, we feel the heat from both sides. We're in danger of a meltdown unless we make time for ourselves.

Take our friend Debbie. She's a totally committed daughter, wife, mother, and "GiGi." If that's not enough, she's starting a home décor boutique and building her dream home.

She's turning in so many different directions she's dizzy. Being an observant friend, Becky noticed Debbie needed to ditch her to-dos and take an afternoon off. Debbie resolved to play hooky the very next day. She realized she couldn't take care of anyone else unless she took care of herself first.

She arranged to meet Becky for shopping. After they split the salmon salad at Brio, their favorite lunch spot, Becky suggested J. Crew for a hip start to the afternoon. It was time Debbie traded in her kitten heels for some fun flip-flops. She also tried on polos, bermudas, flats, even flirty skirts— things she would've never thought about wearing before.

As an extra perk, our shopping star was thrilled to find J. Crew's generous sizing took her from a medium to a small. She walked out with an armload of fabulous finds, even treating herself to a polka-dot pencil skirt that went perfectly with her new hot pink sandals. Indulging, splurging, and being anything but sensible, Debbie succeeded in replenishing both her wardrobe and her spirit.

As Debbie learned, shopping can be a quick fix for restless life syndrome. So, if you find yourself sinking, try shopping!

Girlfriends Rule

It's a girl's prerogative to change her mind, so make sure you know the return policy.

Enjoying Great Escapes

Curing some restless life syndrome cases requires more than an afternoon at the mall. That's when you need the longer-lasting relief a chick trip provides.

Leave the guys home. No boys allowed. Get your girlfriends and run away from it all. Sometimes a change of scenery with friends is necessary to recharge, refocus, and rejoice. (Hallelujah!)

Getting Away with the Girls

Men have been getting away for years. They hunt, fish, and golf, just to name a few. We need to make up for lost time by planning great escapes.

Who goes?—Your aim is comfort, so grab gals you feel a connection with: your sisters, neighbors, sorority friends, anyone with a uterus. But watch your numbers. To keep it manageable, stay under a dozen. More just complicates things.

What to bring—Along with the necessities, pack your patience, flexibility, and sense of humor. Leave the tiaras at home. No queen bees here!

Linda, Charlotte, Terri, Shelley, Debbi, Bev, Debbie, and Becky en route to California.

When to go—Start planning now. Don't wait until you're at the point of no return. We love any excuse for a trip, but sometimes it's easier to get a group together if you plan an annual getaway.

Where to go—Choose a destination with activities everyone enjoys: mega shopping, gallery hopping, and beach plopping are musts for us. Stay tuned for our top diva destinations.

Do the following prep work to get the most from your travel experience:

Put Together a Plan
Your trip will run smoother if you delegate duties. Designate one of the girls as the travel agent to get your trip off the ground. She'll work with the activities director, who checks on concerts, restaurants, spa services, and other options. Together, they'll provide the group with an itinerary that includes flight, hotel, and entertainment information. You'll also need a banker babe with calculator in hand to divvy up restaurant tabs, cab fares, and hotel charges.

Girlfriends Rule

Check your favorite app for the hair weather forecast, so those with issues can arm themselves with an ample aerosol arsenal.

Pack for Your Peeps

Once you know your destination and activities, pack your bags. Every group has someone who is fashion savvy. Tap into her expertise to coordinate your travel wardrobe. She'll eliminate dress stress and embarrassment by helping you choose the right outfit for each occasion. That way you'll avoid showing up in jeans when everyone else is in a strappy sundress. And always, always, pack extra, so you'll have choices and can share with your friends.

Girlfriends Rule

Remember there's no prize for the smallest suitcase on a girlfriend getaway.

Pair Up Similar Roomies

Are you menopausal? Are you an early riser? Do you snore? Are you a party animal? Everyone will be happier and less sleep deprived if you consider these questions when choosing roomies. You can pair up by age, body temperature, modesty levels, or late-night habits. If all else fails, draw straws or get your own room.

Girlfriends Rule

Put high-maintenance divas with low-maintenance gals to ensure everyone has plenty of vanity time.

Make It a Party!

Now is the time to connect with your friends and disconnect from day-to-day responsibilities. Crank up the volume, cause a commotion, and capture the moment. Remember, you're here to make memories, so take plenty of selfies. Let loose, open up, and get close to those special women in your life.

Girlfriends Rule

Limit cell phone time to photos and emergencies during your trip. Save calls, texting, e-mail, and Facebook for later.

Divine Diva Destinations

We've traveled far and wide in search of the perfect backdrop for our girlfriend getaways. From the beach to Broadway, we've researched spots with girlfriends in mind, looking for hotels that cater to sharing. (Our group likes to split everything from sweets to suites.) We love resort towns where everything is at your fingertips, and you don't eat up precious time dealing with trivial details. Big cities with five-star dining, designer shopping, and entertainment options for everyone also top our list.

What's the best setting for getting away with the girls? In the end, we agreed to disagree because we all have different opinions. Most of us like it hot, but some like it cold. Several like it slow, and others like to go, go, go. From lazy to crazy, our favorite diva destinations include:

Grand Cayman: Calm Turquoise Waters Beckon Shelley

Amazing water, abundant marine life, and soft white beaches make Cayman a grand choice. Just an hour flight from Miami, this easy getaway is the perfect spot to relax. Steel drums greet you upon landing, signaling you're now on island time. Head straight to Seven Mile Beach, where you can forget the rest of the world. You can't go wrong choosing the Westin with its champagne-flowing Sunday brunch, impeccable service, vast beaches, and endless water activities. Red Sail Sports can book anything from jet skis to Stingray City excursions. There you can swim with dozens of docile stingrays, feed them, and according to island lore, kiss them for seven years' good luck. This catamaran outing is worth the whole trip.

If you're inclined to shop, grab a cab, especially if you don't want to drive on the left. Head to Georgetown for unbeatable jewelry prices (and no tax). Complete the day with dinner at Casanova's, where you can enjoy great Italian dishes and a breathtaking ocean view, or unwind on the beach at sunset. As Shelley says, "Nothing is better than sipping a tropical drink with your BFFs, knowing you have no place to go and no set time to be there!"

Leave your worries at home, but overpack because you just might decide to call Cayman home.

Girls Gotta Do

1. Take a scuba lesson.
2. Share a Tortuga rum cake.
3. Send a postcard from Hell.

See www.caymanislands.ky for more.

The Gulf Coast: Kiva Keeps Terri Coming Back
If you're longing to leave the hustle and bustle of the city, the beautiful beaches of the Gulf Coast are another great choice. The sugar-white sands and enticing emerald waters from Seaside, Florida to Gulf Shores, Alabama can be an escape to paradise!

Terri's idea of f-u-n (said in a Southern drawl) is to rent a house in a colorful beach community like Kiva Dunes, Alabama's best-kept secret. Here you start the day walking past architecturally unique homes, admiring the swings and rockers on inviting porches.

At the beach, you and your gal pals can soak up the sun, catch up on the latest gossip, and share tropical drinks. After taking in a gorgeous sunset, head to Lucy Buffett's Lulu's (yes, she is Jimmy's baby sister) for her famous fried green tomatoes or to the Original Oyster House for their amazing cheese grits.

Shelley, Linda, Becky, Debbi, Terri, Debbie, and Charlotte take in the gorgeous white-sand beach and clear turquoise water at Kiva Dunes resort, one of the gems on Alabama's Fort Morgan peninsula.

Save time for shopping at the Tanger Outlet in nearby Foley. You can find great deals at Coach, BCBG, Banana Republic, and more. End your trip with a concert under the stars at the Wharf or enjoy the Flora-Bama Lounge's casual vibes. Like the South, everything is slow and easy on a trip to Kiva Dunes.

Girls Gotta Do

1. Catch a throwed roll at Lamberts.
2. Pop into the Pink Pony Pub.
3. Grab anything tie-dyed at the Happy Shak.

See www.kivadunes.com for more.

Palm Springs: Desert Oasis Quenches Debbie's Thirst
Whether you enjoy lounging poolside or shopping until you drop, Palm Springs, California, is a deluxe diva destination. Debbie's favorite full-service resort and spa, the JW Marriott Desert Springs, has everything you need to have fun without fuss. Splurge by renting a convertible, and cruise the eleven miles down Bob Hope Drive to this soothing sanctuary.

From the first glimpse of the palm tree-lined drive, you'll be captivated by its beauty. Pinch yourself—it's not a mirage. A lush exotic oasis awaits, complete with a Starbucks for those who need a jump start in the morning. Pamper yourself with a full day at the spectacular spa, enjoying reflexology, a hot-stone massage, or your choice of services from the extensive menu.

Relax by one of the three sparkling pools with the latest best-seller and a frosty fruity drink. To cool off, head indoors to shop the esplanade for trendy California threads. Catch the gondola in the hotel lobby, and cruise the canal to one of the four signature restaurants. Eat light because you'll want to dance the night away at Costa's, the high-energy nightclub. Later, wind down with a glass of wine around the fire pit.

If you're thirsty for a quick-and-easy getaway, Palm Springs is perfect. Debbie loves escaping to "America's sunshine playground" in February when the daytime temperature hits the mid-70s. But the dry climate ensures a hassle-free hair holiday year-round.

Girls Gotta Do

1. Browse the upscale boutiques on El Paseo.
2. Click close encounters with celebs.
3. Dine under the stars at Pacifica.

See www.visitpalmsprings.com for more.

Santa Fe: Southwestern Tastes & Traditions Entice Becky
Want a destination with great shopping, great margaritas, and great food? Becky recommends Santa Fe, New Mexico, for getting in tune with the arts while getting closer to your girlfriends. Only an hour's drive from Albuquerque, Santa Fe combines cultural experiences and culinary delights with couture shopping.

Choose a hotel within walking distance of the town square, such as the luxurious Eldorado or the quaint Hotel Chimayó de Santa Fe. Don't miss brunch at Cafe Pasqual's, a margarita at the Rosewood Inn of the Anasazi bar, and dinner served by Broadway-singing waiters at La Cantina at La Casa Sena. Then order dessert and a hot toddy at the historic Pink Adobe, the place to see the real Santa Fe. End your evening with a relaxing stroll, enjoying the crisp fresh air with its hint of burning piñon wood (nature's aromatherapy).

You can work off all that food by shopping along the plaza, where Native Americans spread out their handmade treasures for all to see. For those with more expensive tastes, Ortega's on the Plaza offers unique silver-and-turquoise jewelry. You'll find truly funky fashions at the Sign of the Pampered Maiden and vintage-inspired western wear at Cowboys and Indians. And if you're in the market for rustic home furnishings, La Puerta Originals is the place for high-end hacienda-style pieces. Don't forget a trip up Canyon Road. Here you can visit one gallery after another without spending a dime!

A truly satisfying experience awaits you in Santa Fe. You can shop in the summer, ski in the winter, and eat and drink all year long.

Girls Gotta Do

1. Order harvest oatmeal at the Plaza Café.
2. See the Loretto Chapel's miraculous staircase.
3. Play name that tune at Vanessie's Piano Bar.

See www.santafe.com for more.

San Diego: Old-World Charm Captivates Linda
A stone's throw from San Diego, Coronado Island is home to the world-famous Hotel Del. This grand Victorian resort draws you back in time. A national historic landmark built in the late 1800s, it radiates early Hollywood glamour.

The Del sits on one of California's most beautiful beaches, legendary for its glittering gold sand. Combine the hotel's picturesque surroundings with San Diego's year-round ideal weather, and like Linda, you'll say, "This must be heaven."

Clockwise from left: Debbi, Terri, Becky, Linda, Charlotte, and Shelley lunch at The Del.

Start your day with a leisurely stroll around quaint Coronado (with a little luck, you'll catch the Navy SEALs doing their morning workout). Afterward, stop at one of the many sidewalk cafés for a caffeine charge before tackling the sites. First up is a ferry ride to Seaport Village, a charming collection of shops, restaurants, and galleries on the banks of the San Diego harbor. There you can enjoy lunch while admiring the yachts of the oh so rich and famous and take in a colorful local festival.

Later, put on your party clothes and head to the Top of the Hyatt Bar, where sunset is a must. Located on the fortieth floor, high above San Diego Bay, it offers panoramic views of the city that will take your breath away. Try the signature cosmo or a lemon-drop martini; they're delicious works of art. After a toast to friendship, take a quick cab ride to the Gaslamp Quarter downtown for some action. Here you'll find trendy restaurants and lively dance clubs where you can rock and roll. Girls just wanna have fun, and San Diego is a top pick for a fabulous getaway!

Girls Gotta Do

1. Visit the world-class San Diego Zoo.
2. View the sites from an open-air pedicab.
3. Spend an afternoon shopping in chic La Jolla.

See www.sandiego.com for more.

Maui: Drums of the Pacific Beat for Bev

Choice beaches, fine dining, and year-round water activities teamed with perfect weather and friendly locals make Maui the best or as the Hawaiians say, "Maui *no ka 'oi!*"

While plenty of resort options exist, Bev prefers renting a condo on the beach in sunny Kihei. Here you can wake up to songbirds, enjoy coffee on your private lanai overlooking the Pacific, and plan your beach-hopping day. Maui's beaches come in a rainbow of colors—white, black, green, red, and gold. Before heading out, pack a picnic lunch, towels, and loads of sunscreen. Nothing ruins a beach trip quicker than getting sunburned.

If you tire of sand between your toes, swap the cabana for a rental car, and take a day trip to Hana, Haleakala, or Lahaina. The Road to Hana is an adventure involving 620 curves, 59 one-lane bridges, and dozens of spectacular waterfalls. Or, experience the awe-inspiring sunrise at the top of Haleakala, a 10,000-foot dormant volcano. The Valley Isle is also home to the nineteenth-century whaling village of Lahaina. Wear walking shoes on this outing because you'll want to visit every art gallery and souvenir shop housed in the restored Victorian buildings.

Dining is divine on Maui. Nestled in a coconut grove on a secluded white beach in Paia, Mama's Fish House should be your first stop. This pure Polynesian experience serves up the freshest fish with a big helping of aloha-spirit. (You'll want to call ahead for reservations.) Kula Lodge and Restaurant is another favorite. Perched in a tropical garden on Haleakala's western slopes, Kula offers supreme local flavor and unmatched views of the Pacific.

The exotic feel and many ancient traditions make Maui a dream destination. It's hard to believe you don't need a passport, foreign currency or a translator. With no language barrier, the only Hawaiian words you need to know are *aloha* (hello or good-bye) and *mahalo* (thanks).

Girls Gotta Do

1. Take a snorkel trip to Molokini.
2. Pig out at an Old Lahaina Luau.
3. Sip piña coladas at sunset on Kamaole beach.

See www.maui.net for more.

Chicago: The Windy City Blows Debbi Away

If you prefer big city sights, Chicago is a must do. The two major airports close to this vibrant metropolitan area make arrival and departure a breeze. Don't worry about renting a car. Taxis, buses, and trains await your command.

Stay downtown in the heart of the city. You can choose from elegant boutique hotels like the English-inspired Majestic or select luxury accommodations on or near Michigan Avenue. Debbi enjoys the Westin's central location and classic style. You'll love falling into one of their Heavenly Beds after an exciting, yet exhausting, day of exploring.

Michigan Avenue, also known as the Magnificent Mile, is a sight to behold. Take time to notice the beauty of it all. The avenue is lined with garden after garden of seasonal flowers and lovely hanging baskets—quite a contrast to the cement jungle surrounding you.

From the Navy Pier to the American Girl flagship store, this world-famous boulevard includes something for everyone. Get ready to power shop. You can score big bargains at stores like Nordstrom Rack and H&M. Then stop for a mini-makeover at Saks before heading to the upscale fashion-forward boutiques. Treat yourself to a Burberry trench or scarf; you'll need one if you choose to cruise Lake Michigan.

Put your carb-free diet on hold and break for lunch with a slice of deep-dish pizza or fully loaded Chicago dog. Speaking of food (our favorite subject), Chi-town eateries are as plentiful as they are varied. Debbi adores Volare, a cozy Italian restaurant off Michigan Avenue. On a nice evening, it's the perfect place for girlfriends to enjoy this engaging city.

For entertainment, laugh it up at The Second City, marvel at the marine life at the famed Shedd Aquarium, or cultivate your culture at the Joffrey Ballet. Hang on, with so many choices, the Windy City might just blow you away!

Girls Gotta Do

1. Visit around St. Patty's Day when the Chicago River flows green.
2. Carve your name in the wall at Gino's East.
3. Brave the 110-floor elevator ride up the iconic Sears Tower, now known as Willis Tower.

See www.choosechicago.com for more.

New York: The Big Apple Enchants Charlotte

A natural setting for everything from *Breakfast at Tiffany's* to *Sex and the City*, this magic metropolis has it all. Renowned for trendy shopping, elegant dining, award-winning theater, and every type of cultural experience imaginable, New York is a mecca for chick outings. Begin your fairy tale with a stay at the W or the Marriott Marquis in the heart of Times Square. Then it's an easy walk to Fifth-Avenue shopping, Broadway, and the landmark New York Public Library.

If you're a first-timer, take a tour. Gray Line's hop-on hop-off double-decker sightseeing buses are an easy, economical way to go everywhere from Battery Park to Central Park and all points in between. Make Canal Street your first stop for faux Fendis and pretend Pradas. Move on to Greenwich for an eclectic mix of high-end and off-beat shops, antique stores, and quaint cafés.

You can give yourself and your wallet a break by taking in some stunning New York architecture. Catch a panoramic view of the Big Apple from atop the Empire State Building. Visit Grand Central Station, where polished marble staircases and twinkling stars greet travelers from near and far. Enter St. Patrick's Cathedral, the soul of the city, and pause to light a candle for family and friends back home.

Now you're ready for Charlotte's favorite pastime: window shopping along Fifth Avenue. Jimmy Choo, Cartier, and Tiffany are just a few of the glossy designer labels you'll encounter on your way to Central Park. You don't have to buy, but you can dream. Afterward, treat yourself to tea and scones in The Plaza's elegant Palm Court before your horse-and-carriage ride through the heart of Manhattan. You'll share the road with a cross section of New York life: joggers, bikers, and in-line skaters. Have your coachman drop you at the magnificent Metropolitan Museum of Art. On weekend evenings, the gallery crowds are lighter, plus you can enjoy live music.

Later, sip a cosmo in honor of Carrie and the girls at The Monkey Bar in the posh Elysée Hotel. By all means, take in a show at one of Broadway's many world-class theaters. Stop at Carmine's on West Forty-Fourth for an after-theater supper, where girlfriends can split one order of lasagna and still have leftovers.

And don't forget to save room for some of Junior's famous New York cheesecake.

There's no denying New York's appeal. Aptly named the city that never sleeps, this hot, hot, hot melting pot will have you believing in magic!

Girls Gotta Do

1. Join the Today show scene at Rockefeller Center.
2. Marvel at Macy's, the miracle on Thirty-Fourth Street.
3. Order pommes frites at Balthazar's French bistro.

See www.nycgo.com for more.

What are you waiting for? Start making plans for your next trip now. What's the best setting for getting away with the girls? The options are endless. Local or long-distance, simple or spectacular, any destination will do as long as you're making memories with your best girlfriends.

7
Celebrating Life's Ages and Stages

Thong-a-Tude
Celebrations add color, richness, and texture to the fabric of our friendships. Large or small, they strengthen our foundation, weaving us closer together.

It's your birthday! Whether you're turning thirty, forty, fifty, or sixty, you should be looking forward to it. But, big days can bring on big stress. Besides birthdays, graduations, weddings, and new babies (or grandbabies) all come with some anxiety.

How will you commemorate the graduation of your firstborn? Can you help your daughter pull off a wedding with a guest list topping three hundred in three months? What will your grand-child call you? Do you really look like a "mamaw," and when did that happen?

If facing a big day makes your palms sweat, join the club. We've been there, and we've found the secret to keeping your cool is handling the details together.

Savoring the Seasons with Friends

Many women find birthdays difficult. Some would rather cower under the covers or, better yet, just forget about them but not us! We spice things up by putting on our big-girl panties and partying.

Adding Flavor to Plain-Vanilla Birthdays

We make every birthday special, whether it's thirty-one or fifty-three. We relish birthdays as opportunities to shower our friends with love. Early on, planning our celebrations was anything but simple. Although we managed dinners out, cards, and individual cheesy gifts eight times a year, nagging thoughts always peppered the party. "Was everyone called? Did I spend too much or not enough? Where am I supposed to be?"

Organization was obviously the missing ingredient. To stop our stewing, we developed a no-fail recipe to eliminate possible hurt feelings, confusion, and stress.

Terri, Debbie, Debbi, Linda, Becky, Bev, Charlotte, and Shelley make a night of Charlotte's birthday in 2009. Two months later, Charlotte was diagnosed with breast cancer.

The No-Fuss Birthday Blend
Serves: 8

- 1 birthday babe
- 1 perky party planner (the previous birthday babe)
- 6 spicy girlfriends
- 7 sweet or side-splitting sentiments
- 1 beautifully wrapped group gift

The perky party planner calls the birthday babe for her date, time, location, and gift preferences. Then the planner gets the details out via e-mail, e-vite, text, or phone and collects RSVPs. She makes dinner reservations, and then purchases and wraps the present.

On the selected day, she picks up the birthday babe and they meet the spicy girlfriends for mixing and mingling. They share good food, lively conversation, and heartfelt toasts to the honoree. The love and laughter continue as the birthday girl reads her sweet or side-splitting sentiments and opens the beautifully wrapped group gift (usually a gift card of her choice). The evening is topped off with the honoree's favorite dessert (eight spoons included) and a chorus of "Happy Birthday."

To the delight of the waitstaff, the party planner asks for only *one* check and handles payment. Later, she totals the evening's expenses plus the gift and divvies the cost seven ways. (Spicy girlfriends always come prepared to pay.)

Girlfriends Gotta Do

1. Choose a cute card sure to bring a smile to the birthday girl's face.
2. Call her on the big day with birthday blessings.
3. Shower her with love and compliments.

More Candles on the Cake…But Who's Counting?

We advocate seizing the moment and celebrating major milestones to the max! As our theme song says, we "Take It to the Limit" and beyond for those monumental markers. That's when we add zest to the no-fuss birthday blend, turning on the heat to "kick it up a notch" (as Emeril insists) for the big zero birthdays.

Top-Shelf Thirty

Whether your days are spent in a playroom or a boardroom, at thirty, you need to escape reality. Grab your girlfriends and get away to a jammin' concert that sets you free. Dress to impress, and then let loose for the evening. Singing, dancing, and partying like a rock star is a sure cure for your moody blues.

At thirty, we swooned over sexy-hair gods like Steven Tyler and Jon Bon Jovi. Linda, the first in our group to turn thirty, fantasized over crooner Michael Bolton, whose music was her guilty little pleasure. She was first in line to get tickets when she learned his tour included Dallas.

As a bonus, his band was playing in a charity baseball game at the local college the day before the concert. So she plotted to get up close and personal. Her scheme involved sweet talking her husband, Terry, into keeping the kids and enlisting us as the perfect partners in crime. Living her dream, Linda became a Michael Bolton groupie for a day, following his every move on (and off) the baseball field.

We topped off her birthday weekend at his powerful concert, singing along to hits like "Time, Love, and Tenderness" and "When a Man Loves a Woman." What an evening! For those few hours, nothing else mattered. Celebrating with her American idol took away Linda's desperate housewife doldrums. Thanks to this memory marker, she'll never for-get turning the big 3–0.

Girlfriends Gotta Do

1. Split the cost of a stretch limo.
2. Splurge on funky concert T-shirts.
3. Sing and dance in the aisles.

Concerts are a hot ticket whether you're celebrating a birthday or just need some girl time. So Becky, Debbi, Linda, Debbie, Shelley, and Terri had a blast seeing Maroon 5.

Lost-and-Found Forty

Tick. Tick. Tick. Time marches on, and before you know it, you're staring down forty. Your life story now includes some comedy, some drama, and a lot of everyday details.

Where would you be without the girls? Just like angels, they watch over you, making the good times better and the hard times easier. They help you take flight and achieve new dreams. That's why, for us, the symbol of turning forty is a James Avery angel bracelet.

Debbi found herself at a career crossroads at forty. In the midst of corporate turmoil, she would sit at her desk, pondering her next move and thinking, "Should I stay or should I go?"

She prayed for guidance and found herself starting a home-based kitchen-tool business (talk about being out of her element). A few weeks later, Debbi faced a midlife crisis, feeling uncertain, overwhelmed, and pressured. She was trying to balance the needs of two jobs, three kids, and her hardworking husband, Tony. With all this craziness, who had time for a birthday?

But spicy girlfriends never let a birthday slip by without a party. Knowing Debbi needed some extra TLC, we stepped up our plans for her big night. At dessert, we presented her with a circle of seven silver angels to remind her we're linked together and forever friends. That evening, our angel-bracelet tradition was born, and Debbi's career doubts were laid to rest.

This act of love moved Debbi to tears. She was inspired just looking around the table at her personal angels. Bev had been her biggest cheerleader from the start. Shelley had already committed to host party after party to help launch the business. And the rest of us pledged to buy spatulas, spoons, and strainers whether we cooked or not! Besides lifting Debbi's spirits, this encouragement validated her decision to try something different and filled forty with promise.

Girlfriends Gotta Do

1. Order dessert first, preferably chocolate!
2. Laugh till you snort.
3. Always surround yourself with angels.

Fired Up at Fifty

As you approach this milestone, you're gonna be feeling some heat, and it's not all hormonal. The big 5–0 is breathing down your neck, and let's face it, you're not ready to go there. You'll try to deny it, but AARP already has your number.

In our youth, we pictured fifty-year-olds with gray hair, support hose, and deep wrinkles. But the half-century mark no longer has to be frumpy, thanks to L'Oréal, Spanx, and Botox. So why not embrace this stage instead of hiding from it?

It's time to get fired up for the ultimate birthday experience. Follow our lead, and this event will be *all about you*! Start by planning a girlie getaway (get some ideas from Chapter 6), and enlist the help of your BFFs. You'll have a phenomenal celebration if you let your imagination soar.

Here are some surefire ways girlfriends can make turning fifty red hot:

Pull out the stops for a night on the town—Splurge on a chic dress and killer shoes sure to impress.

Dine in style at a trendy restaurant—Begin with a champagne toast and end with a decadent dessert.

Wrap up glamorous gifts—Honor the golden goddess with a jeweled tiara, fluffy red boa, and lacy scarlet thong—all symbols of her eternal hotness.

Charm her with love—Give her a keepsake bracelet adorned with thoughtfully chosen charms to celebrate her exceptional talents.

Speak to her inner beauty—Share heartfelt sentiments, explaining how each charm reflects the birthday girl's impact on your life. (Don't forget the Kleenex.)

Create a time capsule—Provide a red memory box and personalized photo album to store reminders of her special day.

What could be hotter than celebrating the big 5–0 in Las Vegas? This ultimate party destination has it all: internationally themed hotels, five-star dining, and stellar shopping. But it was the lure of big-name entertainment that sent Becky and our band of sisters packing for a long thrill-filled weekend.

After three full days of shopping, eating, and people watching, the most-anticipated night arrived: our date with Celine Dion. We kicked off the party with a private happy hour overlooking the Bellagio's famous dancing fountains.

Gathering around Becky, we began the "charming" ceremony. We crowned her with a stunning tiara, piled on the birthday bling, and presented the coveted bracelet. Then the who-gave-what game began. Memories and tears flowed as Becky matched each charm to a special friend.

"The piano must be from Debbi," she cried, remembering the night they sang old pop favorites around the baby grand at the Hotel Del Coronado.

"Yes!" Debbi squealed, stepping forward. Through laughter and tears, she began reading her tribute to Becky. The short heartfelt letter captured feelings from twenty years of shared memories.

The game continued, one by one, until each charm giver revealed herself. With emotions running high and not a dry eye, we raised our glasses to the newest member of our fiery fifty club.

Next stop…Caesar's Palace. We touched up our mascara and headed down the strip for dinner and the show. Becky looked forward to dining at Mesa Grill secretly hoping to run into Bobby Flay, her celebrity crush. Unfortunately, he wasn't there, but the maître d' was a dead ringer for George Clooney.

"You ladies look lovely tonight," George said as we lingered over coffee and dessert. "You wouldn't be going to see Celine Dion, would you?"

"Yes," we exclaimed in unison, sounding like the Canadian diva's fan club. "How's her show? We hear it's fabulous!"

"I hate to tell you this, but the performance has been cancelled," George said sadly. "Celine has a terrible sinus infection."

Terri and Becky wonder what's next after Celine cancels her show.

"You've got to be kidding me!" Becky cried. "Now what?"

"Let me see what I can do for you girls," George volunteered. He returned a few moments later with VIP passes.

Heads turned as we were whisked through velvet ropes to the front of the line for Caesar's trendiest night club, Pure.

Being dumped by a diva should've turned the evening into a real birthday bust. Instead, Becky hit the jackpot! The red-carpet treatment left her feeling like a star and made turning fifty super hot. We'd love to tell you more, but what happens in Vegas stays in Vegas.

Girlfriends Gotta Do

1. Blow her away with a balloon-filled room.
2. Sing "Happy Birthday" in a very public place.
3. Send her home with a smokin'-hot nightie.

Shakin' Up Sixty and Beyond
Why should turning sixty be a slow dance? Grab your backup babes, and make this a Dreamgirls' moment. They'll help you twist, shout, and shake things up.

It's your time to shine as the leading lady and live your fantasy. We're already making plans. Bev wants to cook like Paula Deen, so we have a Southern culinary class in our future. Linda longs to sip champagne atop the Eiffel Tower while gazing at the City of Light. Shelley has visions of zip lining through Costa Rica's rain forests, so we're getting psyched up for a jungle adventure. (The jury is still out on this one!)

A bigger birthday calls for a bigger memory marker. Make the sky the limit. Don't just dream it, do it.

Girlfriends Gotta Do

1. Wear your age proudly...or lie.
2. Karaoke to music from your favorite decade.
3. Pull an all-nighter (use your imagination).

Breaking Out the Bubbly

Your little pirates and princesses have grown up. Get ready for "Pomp and Circumstance," "Here Comes the Bride," or perhaps "Rock-a-bye Baby." Stress is high. Lists are long. Time is short and your fuses are shorter. So how do you break out the bubbly without losing the fizz?

Turning the Tassel

High school and college graduations are turning points that deserve star treatment. We traditionally honor graduates by creating over-the-top memories. We may not be Verizon, but we've perfected a friends-and-family plan that puts our students on a pedestal for the evening. These special send-offs encourage them to spread their wings without forgetting their roots.

Our celebrations take place around Memorial Day weekend, so we usually have an outdoor theme. We've done all-American cookouts, fun Mexican fiestas, and lively Hawaiian luaus like the one we hosted for Kelli, Terri's daughter.

Kelli was graduating from Colleyville Heritage High School and heading to Abilene Christian University. If she hadn't known better, she would've thought she was in Maui instead of Shelley's backyard.

We greeted her in traditional Hawaiian style, slipping a lei over her head. Tiki torches lit the patio, Don Ho's music filled the air, and colorful hibiscuses adorned the tables.

Being a sand-and-surf kind of girl, Kelli was thrilled with the transformation. A tribute table highlighted her accomplishments from childhood to graduation.

Of course, the menu fit the theme: virgin mai tais, chilled shrimp cocktail, fruit-filled watermelon boats, Linda's kickin' chicken kabobs, teriyaki wild rice, mile-high hula pies, and macadamia nut cookies.

After dinner, we gathered around Kelli as she opened her many presents, including dorm room essentials, reminders of home, and a special strand of pearls from all of us, her extended family. Then it was time for the much-expected grand finale: the college survival kit designed just for Kelli.

Our emcee for the evening, Charlotte's husband, Bob, stepped forward with the humorous-but-helpful gift basket. He opened the tribute by handing Kelli a disposable camera to snap pictures of the village that had helped raise her.

After recalling our girl's tiny beginnings, Bob pulled surprise after surprise from the bag of treats we'd collected to send Kelli off as a college coed. Amid roars of laughter, he used Barbie and Ken props to help her picture her future as a nurse, complete with her own Dr. McDreamy.

Like our graduates before her, this right-of-passage inspired Kelli to take flight. Ready for her college adventure, she packed up her lime-green VW beetle and headed west, feeling secure and ready for whatever the future might bring.

Want to make your high school graduation celebrations a friends-and-family affair? It's easy when you remember the following tips:

Keep it fun and casual—Choose a theme and location sure to please the graduate.

Divvy up the duties—Lighten the load by giving everyone a job: invitations, decorations, and food preparations are a great start.

Roast, boast, and toast—Entertain everyone with anecdotes about the graduate: highlight something funny, something remarkable, and something encouraging.

Share in the gift—Pool your funds for one spectacular group present from the graduate's wish list.

Charlotte, Becky, Linda, Debbi, Debbie, Bev, Terri, Kelli, and Shelley commemorate Kelli's college graduation with a girls-only luncheon.

For our college grads, we follow the parents' lead and the graduate's choice. Some prefer a large parent-hosted party while others choose an intimate lunch with us, their fairy godmothers. In either case, we always honor their pomp and circumstance with a cash gift to help them dress for success.

Party Pointers

1. Make it all about the graduate.
2. Set the mood from the curb to the patio.
3. Honor the parents as well as their child.

Here Comes the Bride

Hearing the words "we're engaged" is music to our ears. Nothing causes us to spring into party-planning action faster than the news of a ring on her finger.

Wedding Belles and Beaus

When the question has been popped and the date set, we whip out our calendars. We have parties to plan, gifts to wrap, and dresses to buy. Peggy Post might tell you it's all about the bride, but what does she know? For us, mothers must share the spotlight! After all, they deal with the inevitable wedding drama, starting with the invitation list.

Limited budgets and potential hurt feelings often leave mothers looking for answers. Should crazy Great-Aunt Sally *and* her newest boy toy be included? Do we really need a cocktail hour, sit-down dinner, and late-night snacks? And what about all those parties?

That's where we, the shower-power team, take charge. After receiving the go-ahead from the mother of the bride (MOB), we get busy. We make it our job to fulfill her wedding belle's dreams. (We'll do much more for the MOB later.)

Does the bride want traditional or trendy? Does she need to stock her kitchen or naughty up her nighties? Should the party be girls only or are boys allowed?

Our belles and beaus have enjoyed crystal and silver teas, wine and cheese tastings, and grill-n-chill parties. But Lesli's limo-and-lingerie girls' night out took the cake!

This precious invitation got everyone revved up for Lesli's limo-and-lingerie party.

Our high-spirited mother-and-daughter group cruised in style from Uptown to Cowtown (Dallas to Fort Worth) in a white stretch limo. With glasses raised, we popped the cork and celebrated our first bride-to-be while traveling to the haute Hotel ZaZa. There, we indulged in cosmos, crudités, and lively conversation in the posh Dragonfly Lounge.

All too soon, we had to return to the limo for the trip to our dinner destination. En route, we presented Lesli with an assortment of naughty nothings and skimpy somethings. A chorus of excited oohs and aahs greeted each gift. Arriving at Fort Worth's cowboy-chic Reata just as the sun set, we stepped from the limo feeling like stars.

Heads turned when our group sashayed into the private party room. Seated around the massive oak table, we experienced a taste of the West, sampling tequila, tamales, and tacos. We topped off our meal with Lesli's favorite dessert: Texas pecan pie and Blue Bell ice cream.

Two-steppin', we made our way back to the limo for a scenic ride through Sundance Square. Lesli popped her head through the sunroof taking in the bright lights of the big city as we all sang "Going to the Chapel." Feeling showered with love, our radiant bride-to-be tossed her cares into the night and fixed her sights on the big day.

Stuck choosing a theme for your bridal shower? Consider the following:

Isn't It Romantic?—Decorate with pearls and lace for an old-fashioned feel like we did for Debbie's daughter, Lauren. Serve petit fours, truffles, and tea sandwiches on grandmother's china. Send the vintage bride home with love notes from the guests.

Two to Tango—Fill glass hurricanes with chili peppers and sunflowers, float sombreros in the pool, and add colorful lights to complete the ambiance. Dish up guacamole, chicken enchiladas, and refried beans. Have guests share their "hot tips" for a spicy marriage.

Turn Up the Heat—Create a cozy kitchen atmosphere with copper pots, a fresh fruit-and-vegetable centerpiece, and the aroma of homemade apple pie. Whip up comfort foods like fried chicken, mac-n-cheese, and chocolate chip cookies. Ask friends to bring their favorite recipe, and sign his-and-hers aprons as keepsakes.

Destination Honeymoon—Set the stage with the couple's getaway in mind. If they're bound for Paris, display travel books, old passports, and bag tags in small trunks. Pour champagne and pass french pastries and fancy hors d'oeuvres. Say bon voyage to the happy couple by presenting a map of good wishes signed by all.

Once you have your theme, take inventory. You can often cover party needs by shopping your friends' cupboards. Who has a crystal punch bowl? Who has white tablecloths? Who has matching serving dishes? By combining your efforts and resources with a little ingenuity, you can throw a party worthy of both the bride-to-be and Martha Stewart.

Party Pointers

1. Keep bridezilla at bay by consulting her.
2. Limit stress by staging the shower early.
3. Reward yourself with a post-party toast.

TLC for the MOB

As the big day approaches, the mother of the bride is often overwhelmed and underappreciated while still searching for the perfect dress. To keep your composure, you need some tender loving care and support from your girlfriends.

Gone are the days when the mother of the bride *always* wore a traditional wedding suit. As the second most-watched person at the wedding (sorry groom), today's MOB wants a dress that's anything but matronly. Your look must be flattering, fashionable, and fun!

Above left, Bev, Becky, Shelley, Linda, and Debbie; right,
Charlotte and Debbi gather round gorgeous mother of the bride,
Terri, at the wedding of her oldest daughter, Stephanie.

To find the mother of all dresses, plan on doing the following:

Bring your entourage—Don't shop alone. Grab friends with fashion sense who know the top shops and will make it an event not a chore. (Shopping where champagne is served helps.)

Follow the bride's vision—The wedding location, time of day, and season all affect your selection. Is it in a chapel or on a beach? Is it in the afternoon or after five? Are tulips blooming or leaves falling?

Play up your assets—Got great legs? Show them off. Blessed with an hourglass figure? Choose a formfitting design. Have sculpted arms? Bare them in a strapless number.

Consider your color—Pick a hue that's good for you and the wedding party (you want to complement, not clash, with the bridesmaids). Communicate with the mother of the groom, and be sure to save white for the bride.

Polish your look—Pamper yourself by hiring a professional for hair and makeup. Classic jewelry, trendy (but feet friendly) heels, and a small evening bag complete the picture.

Remember, you want to be a head turner not a showstopper. Check the mirror to make sure your 360-degree view skirts any wardrobe malfunction. Think elegant, not flashy, and go for a look that lasts. It's going to be a long night.

MOB's Gotta Do

1. Spanx any lumps, bumps, and bulges.
2. Practice, practice, practice in your wedding heels.
3. Keep smiling for a strong photo finish.

It's Marry Time

When the big day finally arrives, you may be tempted to micro-manage. But the MOB can't be everywhere at once. Send out an SOS to your BFFs for help handling last-minute details and calming your nerves.

Talk about last minute. Even our über-organized Shelley had to call for bridal backup before her daughter Lindsey tied the knot.

Wanting to make sure she had all the nuptial necessities, Shelley ran through her list with Becky, an experienced MOB. Becky suggested wearing waterproof mascara, using transparent deodorant, and most importantly, breaking in the wedding shoes.

So Shelley breezed into the rehearsal wearing three-inch heels, thinking she had it all under control. But by the end of the evening, her soles were under siege. She realized she'd have to squeeze an emergency shopping trip into an already packed wedding-day schedule.

Early the next morning, Shelley woke from a shoe night-mare to a panicked Lindsey moaning, "Mom, my arm is numb. I can't feel anything."

Shelley, fearing the worst, rushed Lindsey to the nearest doc-in-the-box only to find the wait was more than an hour.

Having no time to spare, Shelley called Terri, the hotline to our favorite family physician. After reassuring Shelley, ever-calm Terri handed the phone to her husband, Dr. Mike.

"Don't worry," Mike said in his usual comforting manner. "I'll meet you at my clinic in ten minutes."

After a quick examination, he treated Lindsey for a pinched nerve, not a heart attack. With a smile, he prescribed shots all around: Toradol for Lindsey and tequila for Shelley.

"See you at the wedding," he said, sending them on their way.

With that emergency handled, Shelley was free to focus on her feet and her next stop—Nordstrom's shoe department. She quickly scanned the dress pumps, eyeing a pair of black-patent peep toes with a manageable heel.

"Will these work?" she wondered, reaching for her cell phone. "Linda will know."

"Why are you at the mall?" Linda shrieked when she answered the call. "Shouldn't you be at the church by now?"

"Yes, but I'm having a shoe crisis," Shelley cried. "Can I wear patent in the fall?"

"Absolutely. Patent is perfect year-round," Linda replied. "Get 'em and go!"

With the choice made, Shelley whipped out her credit card, bought the shoes, and raced for the door. Disaster averted. Thanks to her friends, the rest of the evening was smooth sailing, both down the aisle and across the ballroom floor.

Debbi, Becky, Linda, Charlotte, Shelley's future son-in-law, Ross, Shelley's daughter, Lindsey, Debbie, and Terri enjoy Lindsey's bridal shower.

To keep your wedding wits about you, delegate, delegate, delegate. Recruit friends to help you handle the following to-dos:

Dress the entry table—Start with elegant linens, the guestbook, and several pens. Then, as space allows, add personal touches such as a wedding portrait, family Bible, and decorative candles. We also display keepsake crosses carefully selected by each of us to honor the happy couple.

Pick up snacks for the belles and beaus—Keep your troops from dropping at the altar by providing bottled water and light snacks. Serve cheese, grapes, and plain crackers. Save the chocolate and alcohol for the reception.

Be your beck-and-call girls—Ask two trusted friends to be your extra hands. Have the right-hand gal check last-minute details, like making sure all the battle stations are manned. Use the left-hand girl to handle lip gloss, hairspray, and other touch-ups to prepare you for final inspection.

Make a sweep of the dressing rooms—Before heading to the reception, collect purses, curling irons, and clothes left by the wedding party. Stash the loot in someone's car and deal with it the next day.

Put friends in charge, so you can focus on the joy of the occasion. Turning over the details will put you at ease and have you toasting a mission accomplished at the end of the evening.

MOB's Gotta Do

1. Create a wedding guidebook covering every last detail.
2. Survey your friends to match talents to tasks.
3. Recruit, delegate, and then celebrate!

"I'm Too Young to Be a Grandma!"

You can't help but wonder how it's possible that your baby is having a baby when you hear the sweet words, "I'm expecting." Then your mothering instinct takes control, and your mind starts racing. When does the nursery need to be ready? Will I be buying Barbies or baseballs? Will spoiling be allowed?

But take it from us, your girlfriends just want to know if you'll be a traditional Grandma or a trendy GiGi. Will you be hands-on or hands-free? Will you rock the little one to sleep or let them self soothe? Will you sneak sweet treats or offer organic edibles? (And by the way, what on earth is a Bumbo?)

Our group of groovin' grandmothers has latched onto these names: Bev (Gum-Gum), Shelley (Mimmy), Terri (Grammi), Debbie (GiGi), Becky (Ah-Rah), and Debbi (Gramma). As of printing time, Charlotte and Linda were grandma wannabes.

Now is your chance to lay claim to a name that reflects your personality. What's it going to be?

Rooted in Tradition
If you're a sentimental soul who's more comfortable with a time-honored title, these names are for you:

Abuela	Mamaw
Gammy	Mawmaw
Gram	Memaw
Gram-Gram	Mimi
Gramma	Momer
Grammi	Nana
Gramsie	Nanny
Grandma	Ninnie
Grand-mamá	Nonie
Grand-mére	Nonna
Grandmother	Oma
Granny	

Terms of Endearment
Maybe you're the affectionate type who showers loved ones with hugs and kisses. Then you could be one of the following:

Angel	Dearie
Bon-bon	GiGi
Bunny	Gum-Gum
Cookie	Honey
Cutie	Jammi

Kiki	Mimsie
Kitty	Minnie
Lolli	Peaches
Lovey	Precious
Meegee	Sugar
Mimmy	Sunni
Mims	Sweetie

Straight from Hollywood

Perhaps you're livin' in the fast lane and need a name that screams cool, hip grandmother like one of these:

Babe	Glammi
Bebe	Jewel
Belle	Lala
Blossom	Lulu
ChaCha	Mamma Mia
Diva	Mombo
Dolly	Porsche
Fanci	Queenie
FiFi	Sassy
G.G. (Gorgeous Grandma)	Tootsie
GaGa	YaYa

Choosing the perfect grandmother name can prove labor intensive. But have fun and don't overthink it. Sometimes you have to try on a name to see if it fits. Becky's first choice, Gammy, was pooh-poohed by her daughter Paige, so now Becky's answering to Ah-Rah.

Be prepared…your sweet grandchildren will probably put their spin on your choice. And the minute they do, your heart will melt, and you will become the name.

Gram's Gotta Do

1. Pick your name quickly, so you have first dibs.
2. Don't fret if Hallmark has no card for your name.
3. Be you first and Gram second.

Bring on the Baby Blowout

Today's baby showers are chic events. The mother-to-be (MTB) proudly parades her baby bump while wearing five-inch heels. Her registry includes monogrammed bibs, upscale diaper bags, and BOB, the Cadillac of jogging strollers. Her sophisticated palette calls for hummus, gourmet cupcakes, and virgin cosmos instead of yesterday's onion dip, sheet cake, and sparkling punch.

Bring on the baby blowout! The modern MTB inspires us to tap into our creativity and move from pastels to richer hues, from the predictable to the unexpected. Here are some rockin' ideas for showering millennium moms:

Guess the Sex

With more and more expectant couples knowing their baby's sex, many are having preshowers to include friends and family in the "big reveal." For this party, ask guests to forecast their prediction by wearing pink or blue while honorees wear white.

Order a two-layer white-on-white cake with a pink or blue filling. Keep the big news hush-hush by having someone in the know call the bakery with the top-secret color. Make the cake the focal point when decorating for the party.

As guests arrive, build anticipation by allowing them to buy in to a just-for-fun "baby pool," predicting the newborn's birth date and weight. All money collected goes to the diaper fund. At announcement time, separate the pinks from the blues, and let the cake cutting begin. Have the parents-to-be slice through the layers together, and then raise the server to reveal the baby's sex.

Gaga for Green

Besides thinking pink or blue, today's moms think green. That means incorporating concern for the planet in all aspects of your event. How? Recycle, reduce, and reuse.

- Save postage and save a tree by sending e-vites instead of paper invitations. Check out the options at www.evite. com.
- Reduce waste by using real dishes and decorating with stuffed animals, cute containers, and other items that will find a home in baby's nursery.
- Lessen pollution by encouraging guests to wrap gifts in reusable materials, such as cloth diapers, receiving blankets, and hooded towels. Also, suggest they attach a book for baby's library or a bow for baby's hair instead of purchasing a card.

Stuffed animals for baby's nursery played a starring role in the decorations for our Winnie the Pooh-themed shower for Bev's daughter-in-law, Lindsey.

Sip 'n See

When it's time to ooh and aah, a Sip 'n See is a grand way to show off the baby to family and friends. This Southern-inspired, first-peek-at-the-newborn serves as a more personal birth announcement. It works especially well after adoptions, after difficult pregnancies, or with proud parents from out of town.

Unlike a shower, this come-and-go gathering can be given by the grandparents. Invite entire families to join in the celebration. Serve canapés, tea cakes, and other fancy finger foods on your good china. Dress the wee ones in their Sunday best...after all, they *are* the main attraction. Remember presents are optional, but best wishes and baby kisses are required.

Gifts for Gram

A baby onboard has a huge ripple effect, and may rock the boat for proud grandparents as well as new parents. To help smooth the waters, we make it a practice to honor the all-important grandmother with a little shower that we like to call a "sprinkling." We keep it small because most grandmothers need only the bare necessities for Gram-and-me time.

Make it an intimate affair with her closest friends. Go light on the food; heavy on the fun. Serve champagne and cupcakes, wine and cheese, or depending on her style, longnecks and nachos. Bring gifts to stock Gram's own baby basket, such as books, blocks, and burp cloths. This simple, relaxing moment provides the calm before the storm.

What makes our baby showers unique? We like to honor the grandmother-to-be as well as the little mother. After a successful soiree, we carry the mood over to a grand finale toasting one of our own.

Following Angelina's shower, we continued the fun by surprising her mom, Debbi, with a "sprinkling." We said good-bye to the last guest and loaded Angel's SUV with the baby's bounty. Then it was time to kick off our shoes and start the after party.

While Becky poured the bubbly, Bev brought out our treats: sea-salt bagel chips, her signature hot pepper peach cheese ball, and the leftover party petit fours. Linda ushered Debbi to the place of honor, and we surrounded her with pink-themed grandbaby gifts.

Teary-eyed and grateful, Debbi thanked us saying, "How precious! This makes it feel so real. Y'all have made sure I'm ready for my sweet little granddaughter."

What a magical moment! We all felt blessed to have shared in our dear friend's joy.

Anything goes for today's moms. By taking these baby-blow-out ideas and making them your own, you become a part of welcoming in the next generation. Could anything be more rewarding?

Girlfriends Gotta Do

1. Cater to the little mother's quirky cravings.
2. Poll guests for their top parenting tips.
3. Create a visual with vintage baby photos.

Embracing Pinch-Me Moments

We all have times that seem almost too good to be true. Moments that can take your breath away, make your heart skip a beat, and bring tears of joy to your eyes.

Some feel the pinch-me moments when falling in love and getting married, when becoming a parent, and one day, when holding their first grandchild. Others experience that high climbing to the top of the Statue of Liberty, seeing the sunset from the cliffs in Santorini, or getting stuck in an elevator with Bradley Cooper (*every* woman's fantasy). For us, seeing our dreams realized in completing this book was the crowning glory. That was a pinch-me moment times eight!

Focus on the Feeling

You don't have to leave home to feel the thrill. Any moment that seems larger than life qualifies, whether you're savoring an unexpected Christmas Eve snowfall or finding that perfect pair of jeans that make your butt look fabulous. These mini pinch-mes happen every day. Just open your eyes. Sometimes the smallest things can give you the biggest lift. So big, you want to hang on to them forever.

Looking back, we had several magical moments one September night when meeting at Charlotte's to work on our book. It was supposed to be all business. After all, the guys had gone hunting, and we had the night to write. We had planned to order pizza, but food wasn't the first thing on our minds.

> *Charlotte was excited to show us her newest bedroom find: an elegant, espresso leather bench. After agreeing she had made the perfect purchase, our decorating divas went into high gear tweaking the room. Linda started fluffing and rearranging the symmetrical pillows to give the bed that wow factor. Bev and Debbie suggested adding finishing touches like brooches and buttons.*

The more they did, the more excited Charlotte became. It was like Genevieve Gorder, Martha Stewart, and Candice Olson were in her bedroom having a professional powwow! This boudoir blitz turned out to be the first of the evening's many pinch-mes.

Heavenly smells brought us back to earth. The aroma of basil and garlic sent Bev rushing to the kitchen to pull her bubbling basil pesto bruschetta from the oven. While she served her Italian masterpiece, Becky poured the Pinot Noir. With the explosion of flavors igniting our senses, all we wanted to do was savor the moment and beg for Bev's recipe.

Wine wasn't the only thing flowing that night. The words poured out as we laughed, shared, and revisited old times, reliving past pinch-mes. What a great feeling! Our creative juices were at an all-time high, exceeding even our expectations for the evening. (No writer's block that night!)

What made this meeting so extraordinary? Some things can't be explained. All we had to do was show up, slow down, and embrace the moment. That's the way pinch-mes often happen. The best ones are unplanned.

In our hurried, stressed-out lives, it's easy to overlook mini pinch-mes. We encourage stopping to feel the woo-hoos instead of running to check off to-dos. You have permission to scratch the schedule. Sometimes you have to give up control and give in to spontaneity.

Girlfriends Gotta Do

1. Appreciate everyday moments.
2. Journal your joy.
3. Share pinch-mes on Facebook, Twitter, and Instagram.

Livin' Larger Than Life

It's good to be here.

Time has given us wisdom and insight (along with a few gray hairs!) We feel more empowered, confident, and determined. And it shows. Together, we've seen a dream materialize. Thirty years ago, we never imagined ourselves working together, let alone writing a book about our friendship.

Get Ready for a Reality Check

Some of us have downsized, simplified, and decluttered. Meanwhile, others have stepped out, building vacation hideaways, completing college degrees, and shifting gears into new careers.

What's driving these life-changing choices? Consider the following:

The unavoidable curse of aging—Although we've lived half our lives, we're not ready to be "old." We may have whacked-out hormones (we even cry over Maxwell House commercials), but we'll always be boomer babes!

The kids have flown the coop—We've become empty nesters (at least until they come back to roost while adjusting their course). We spent years as Sunday school teachers and soccer moms. Now we need to spread our wings and enjoy a new identity.

We've turned into our parents—Yikes, talk about role reversal. Now we're the grownups! Ready or not, we're in charge of everything from taking dad to the doctor to making mom's famous Thanksgiving dressing.

We're living in a technology-driven domain—We have a love/hate relationship with modern devices. While breathing new life into some careers, these advances suck the air out of others. The Samsung Galaxy, iPad, and Microsoft Surface simplify our lives, but at what cost? They keep us feeling wired in a wireless world.

We've had some unwelcome wake-up calls—Failed relationships, financial setbacks, and final farewells have impacted all our lives. And, of course, we haven't escaped the mother of them all, the Big C. Two of us—that's 25 percent—have faced the nightmare of breast cancer.

Don't Think You're Immune
In life, you have many highs and lows. Savor those perfect pinch-mes because you never know when a please-wake-me-from-this-nightmare moment is around the corner.

Our dear, sweet Linda hit rock bottom at forty-six when a half-dollar-sized lump sent her spiraling into a personal nightmare. A phone call from the doctor had just confirmed her greatest fear: breast cancer.

"How could this be happening to me?" Linda thought. "I should be low risk."

As her legs turned to Jell-O, she began a quick mental inventory:

- *No family history…Check.*
- *Late onset of menstruation…Check.*
- *Breastfed my babies…Check.*
- *Never missed a mammogram…Check.*
- *Feeling good with no symptoms…Check (well, except for that strange muscle-like lump).*

In a split second, her life as she knew it was over. She felt overwhelmed, helpless, and betrayed by her body.

To make matters worse, she received the news on her son's fourteenth birthday. How ironic to be celebrating Jonathan's life as she felt her life slipping away. He'd been looking forward to dinner at Benihana for weeks. Linda barely had time to confide in her husband, Terry, before putting on a happy face and faking it. Terry's quiet strength carried her through the evening.

Linda could not escape the Big C; it suddenly consumed her. She couldn't sleep, couldn't eat, and couldn't breathe but forced herself to keep going because she had decisions to make and appointments to arrange. Breast surgeons, plastic surgeons, and oncologists. Bone scans, MRIs, and PET scans. Double mastectomy, bilateral reconstruction, expanders, and implants. Chemotherapy, radiation, and even more scans. Linda had too much to absorb. She felt as if people were speaking a foreign language.

Linda chose an aggressive attack: a double mastectomy, TRAM flap reconstruction, and four rounds of cancer-zapping chemotherapy. Fighting for normalcy, she returned to work as quickly as possible after surgery and continued working full-time during treatment. Her job provided a temporary diversion; it was the one thing she could control.

For the next two years, Linda put on an award-winning all-is-well act. She wore a brave face to protect her family. They didn't deserve to suffer because she'd been thrown into a deep, dark pit. After all, Jonathan was adjusting to junior high, Terry's job kept him on the road, and their daughter, Emily, was finding her way as a college freshman three hours from home.

Keeping things normal was a constant struggle. Linda felt like she was having an out-of-body experience, smiling on the outside while screaming on the inside. Only her strong faith in God and the support of her family and friends helped her get from one day to the next.

When our fifteen-plus-year survivor looks back, she realizes this traumatic ordeal forever changed her. Today, Linda is stronger and more aware of every blessing. She's also compelled to reach out to others by sharing these powerful life lessons:

We are not in control!—God is. He has plans for all of us, and His plans are perfect.

Faking it can help you make it—Resist the urge to run and hide in your cave.

It's OK to lean on family and friends—They can be a safe haven, loving you even when you don't feel very loveable.

In life, no one gets a trouble-free guarantee—Bad things do happen to good people.

Each day is a gift from God, so start with a prayer—"Thank you, God, for this day. Please don't let me waste a moment."

Just Say Yes!
Standing up to the Big C convinced Linda to start livin' larger than life. She began embracing a more adventurous outlook, taking her world from black-and-white to Technicolor. In fact,

she erased the word no from her vocabulary. Instead of feeling trapped by routine, she started following her impulses and saying yes without hesitation.

As Stephen Colbert says, "Saying yes begins things. Saying yes is how things grow." So Linda was even inspired to start a "say yes" list, including all the things in life she didn't want to miss. She wrote down thrills she wanted to experience (hot-air ballooning in New Mexico), sights she longed to see (the sun rising over Mount Haleakala), and skills she dreamed of mastering (J. Lo's smokin'-hot dance moves).

She started checking off these gotta dos one by one, beginning by escaping to Hawaii to create memories with her family. There they marveled at nature and celebrated life while clinging to each other. What a special moment in time!

Loving that feeling of accomplishment, Linda began planning her next adventure. That set the tone for her continually evolving "say yes" list. She checks off one gotta do and then immediately adds another.

Linda's contagious new attitude and excitement for life soon infected our entire group. We began examining our hopes and dreams, asking ourselves, "Do we really need to face a personal crisis before we wake up and reach for more?"

"N-o," we all answered emphatically and started our own "say yes" lists:

Becky   wants to make it to the top of the most famous rock formation in Yosemite, so she can legitimately buy the "I hiked Half Dome" T-shirt. She also longs to see *The Last Supper* in Milan and to begin writing a children's book about her sweet dachshunds, Allie and Emmie.

Bev   dreams of living on an authentic Hawaiian plantation for months at a time, experiencing the island culture, and growing her own Plumeria to turn into fragrant leis. She also looks forward to the day when she can educate her granddaughter in the fine art of riding roller coasters.

Charlotte   fantasizes about being part of New York's fabulous Fashion Week. Inspired by two of her favorite films, *French Kiss* and *Under the Tuscan Sun*, she also says "*Oui, oui*" to traveling the French Riviera and "*Salute*" to mastering Italian cuisine.

Debbi   yearns to bike through the New England countryside in the fall. She also wants to follow in the footsteps of Jesus by taking a spiritual journey to Israel that ends in the Holy City of Jerusalem and dreams of ministering with Samaritan's Purse international relief.

Debbie   would love to throw her cautious nature to the wind and experience the thrill of a spontaneous adventure. She also has her sights set on traveling to Monaco, the playground of the rich and famous, and (believe it or not) taking up the electric guitar.

Shelley   pictures herself in Africa, serving on a mission team. She hopes to someday sail the Caribbean on a fully staffed catamaran for *at least* a month. She also plans to complete her divemaster certification, so one day she and her husband can retire on an island and teach scuba for fun.

Terri   sees herself leavin' on a jet plane, following musicians like Steely Dan and Justin Timberlake wherever they play. When she touches down, she wants to hit the road, exploring everything from thrift stores to antique malls for unexpected treasures.

As we revealed our dreams, we were amazed to discover each other's suppressed desires. We thought we knew our girlfriends inside and out. What a surprise! Who would've guessed the deep-seated passions just waiting to be unleashed?

Today, we look at each other with a fresh set of eyes. Instead of slowing us down, age has revved us up. We want more out of life and our girlfriends get it. We've *always* been each other's biggest cheerleaders. Now our friendships give us the confidence and support to set our dreams in motion.

Clockwise from left: Shelley, Debbie, Becky, Debbi, and Charlotte quickly said "Oui!" when Linda, front, suggested a trip to Paris.

Become a Daydream Believer

We urge you to find what stirs your heart—those pinch-me moments that help you live larger than life. Start by taking a long look in the mirror. Examine your wants and needs as well as your regrets, fears, and unfulfilled desires. Jot down your thoughts to build your own "say yes" list. Prioritize as you go and include everything from simple pleasures to your wildest fantasies.

Do you secretly long to be on *Dancing with the Stars?* Tackle the tango, and then synchronize the swing. Enjoy spending time in the kitchen and sharing clever culinary tips? Cook up a YouTube video to feed your foodie addiction. Love men in uniform, the national anthem, and fireworks on the Fourth of July? Put your patriotic personality to work for the USO.

Have fun planning. Stretch your imagination and don't stress over the details. Answers can be as close as a Google search. After doing your homework, jump into action, and enjoy the journey.

Girlfriends Gotta Do

1. Make your "say yes" list real by making it known.
2. Include a friend (or even seven) in your escapades.
3. Celebrate each victory in a big way.

Saying yes and checking off your gotta dos one by one will fuel your fire to see and do all the things you've been saving for tomorrow. That's when being red thong strong means livin' larger than life!

Now that our secrets are out, we challenge you to buy a little red thong, grab your girlfriends, and leave your troubles and granny panties behind.

Entertaining Favorites

Special events call for special foods. Here are some proven winners sure to *wow* your guests.

Fruittinis
By Linda

Warm-weather parties call for light, refreshing drinks like these herb- and fruit-infused waters. Fresh mint or basil gives them an amazing flavor while fruit supplies just the right amount of sweet tang. Be creative with your combinations...both your taste buds and your waistline will thank you!

Strawberry, Orange, and Lime with Mint Fruittinis

- 4 to 6 strawberries, hulled, and quartered
- ½ lime, sliced thin

- ½ orange, sliced thin
- Small handful fresh mint (or basil)
- 1 orange, sliced thin, for garnish

Watermelon-and-Basil Fruittinis

- 2 slices watermelon, cut into thirds or quarters plus small slices for garnish
- Small handful fresh basil, scrunched slightly to release flavor

Fill a clear-glass juice pitcher with ice. Place fruit on top of ice. Drop in a small amount of mint or basil and cover with water.

Let water infuse at least an hour to release the flavors of your fruit and herbs.

Serve the strawberry-orange-lime fruittinis in pretty wine or martini glasses, garnishing the rims with orange slices. Offer watermelon-and-basil fruittinis in small mason jars trimmed with a bit of watermelon.

Basil Pesto Bruschetta
By Bev

No matter how you say it, everyone agrees this crunchy Italian appetizer is fantastico! Use fresh herbs and vegetables, pile on the toppings, and serve with forks, so you can savor every last crumb.

- 1 french baguette, cut diagonally into ½-inch thick slices
- 1 tablespoon extra virgin olive oil
- ½ cup diced fresh mushrooms
- 2 to 3 seeded and diced fresh roma tomatoes
- Basil pesto
- Fresh mozzarella cheese, sliced ⅛-inch thick and large enough to fit each bread slice
- Fresh basil leaves

Set oven on broil.

Brush both sides of the baguette slices generously with olive oil. Place on a cookie sheet and toast both sides lightly. Lower the oven to 300°F.

Sauté diced mushrooms and tomatoes in olive oil until soft but not mushy. Drain excess juices from mixture and set it aside.

Spread a small amount of pesto on one side of the toasted bread. Top each with a mozzarella slice followed by 1 teaspoon of the mushroom-tomato mixture.

Return the bruschetta to the oven and leave in just until the cheese begins to soften. Remove and top each slice with a basil leaf. Serve immediately.

Easy Baked Brie
By Debbie

A family favorite, this delicious hors d'oeuvre makes a festive statement at parties and holiday gatherings. Serve garnished with rosemary sprigs and fresh cranberries and surrounded by hearty crackers.

- 1 sheet frozen puff pastry
- 1 large brie, rind removed
- ¼ cup chopped candied pecans or honey-roasted almonds
- ¼ cup dried cranberries
- Brown sugar for sprinkling
- 1 egg white mixed with 1 tablespoon water (egg wash)

Thaw the puff pastry just enough, so you can work with it easily. Place brie in the center of the pastry and top with nuts and dried cranberries. Sprinkle with brown sugar.

Fold the puff pastry over the brie, seal edges, and brush with the egg wash. Bake according to the directions on the puff pastry box.

Hot Pepper Peach Cheese Ball
By Bev

Warning—this creamy peach-flavored cheese ball is addictive. Its perfect combination of sweet-and-spicy flavors leaves guests begging for more. You can shake things up a bit by using other hot pepper jellies such as raspberry or plum.

- 2 (8-ounce) bricks cream cheese, softened
- ⅓ cup hot pepper peach jelly
- 1 tablespoon grated onion
- 1 cup shredded monterey jack cheese

Place first three ingredients into food processor and pulse until thoroughly mixed.

Spread the monterey jack on a sheet of wax paper then dump the cream cheese mixture on top of it. Form into a ball and roll, covering entirely with monterey jack cheese. Wrap the ball tightly with wax paper and put in a plastic storage bag. Refrigerate overnight. Serve with bagel chips.

Mexican Corn Dip
By Terri

Great for a crowd, this quick-and-easy Tex-Mex starter works for everything from tailgating to cocktail parties. Serve it with blue, red, or green corn chips to up the fun factor.

- 2 (11-ounce) cans Green Giant Mexicorn, drained
- 1 (4-ounce) can chopped green chilies, drained
- 4 to 6 green onions, chopped
- 1 (16-ounce) container sour cream
- 2 cups shredded cheddar cheese

Mix all ingredients well and refrigerate. Best when chilled overnight.

Zesty Guacamole
By Charlotte

Fresh-squeezed lime juice makes this guac rock. If you can't find soft avocados, buy green ones, wrap them in a dish towel, and set them in your pantry or another dark place to ripen. Check their progress daily because they can turn to mush quickly if you're not careful.

- 4 small avocados, peeled and pitted (save one of the seeds if not serving immediately)
- ¼ cup chopped, fresh cilantro
- ¼ teaspoon onion powder
- 2 tablespoons salsa
- 4 tablespoons fresh-squeezed lime juice (about 2 limes)
- 1 tablespoon diced pickled jalapenos
- ⅛ teaspoon sea salt
- Freshly ground black pepper to taste

Mash the avocados with a fork or pastry blender. Add remaining ingredients. Stir to mix well.

Make ahead tip: This tasty dip can be prepared one or two hours in advance if stored in the refrigerator with the reserved avocado seed inserted in the mixture. Remove seed before serving.

Ham and Spinach Quiche
By Debbi

Whether served for brunch, lunch, or a light supper, this yummy ham, spinach, and cheese pie is always a big hit. Complete the meal with soup, fruit, or a tossed salad.

- 1 (9-inch) unbaked pie shell
- 1 egg white
- 2 slices swiss cheese (7 x 4-inch)
- 1 (10-ounce) package frozen, chopped spinach, thawed and drained
- 4 fresh mushrooms, sliced
- 1 thick-cut slice deli ham, cut into cubes
- 3 eggs, beaten
- 1 cup half-and-half
- 2 teaspoons flour
- ½ teaspoon salt
- ¼ cup shredded cheddar cheese

Preheat oven to 350°F.

Brush bottom and sides of crust with egg white. Place swiss cheese on pie crust. Then layer spinach, mushrooms, and ham. Mix next 4 ingredients. Pour into pie shell. Sprinkle with cheddar cheese. Bake 40 to 45 minutes or until knife comes out clean. Makes 4 to 6 main dish servings.

Kickin' Chicken Kabobs
By Linda

These Asian-inspired bites are perfect for a backyard pool party or Hawaiian-themed shower. Packed with flavor, they're sure to please even the pickiest eater.

Marinade

- 6 tablespoons soy sauce
- 6 tablespoons brown sugar
- 4 tablespoons sherry or rice vinegar
- 2 tablespoons sesame oil
- ½ teaspoon ginger powder (or 1 teaspoon freshly grated ginger)
- ½ teaspoon garlic powder (or 1 teaspoon fresh garlic, minced)
- 2 tablespoons cornstarch

Kabobs

- 8 skinless, boneless chicken breast halves, cut into 2-inch pieces
- 1 (20-ounce) can pineapple chunks, drained (or fresh pineapple cut into chunks)
- Skewers

Mix all marinade ingredients, except cornstarch, reserving half to make a basting sauce. Put chicken pieces and half the marinade in a ziplock bag, place in refrigerator for several hours or overnight, and turn occasionally.

Put reserved marinade in a small saucepan. Dissolve cornstarch in ¼ to ⅓ cup water and add to the mixture. Heat on the stove, boiling lightly, until sauce thickens. Set aside.

Lightly oil grill grate. Thread chicken and pineapple onto skewers. (If using wood skewers, soak in water to prevent burning.)

Grill 15 to 20 minutes, turning occasionally, until chicken juices run clear. Brush with basting sauce during the last few minutes of grilling.

Serve on a bed of brown rice, and garnish with fresh chopped parsley or cilantro.

Almond Poppy Seed Bread
By Debbi

One bite of this luscious treat will have your guests coming back for more and more and more. Who knew almond extract could have such a powerful effect on your taste buds?

Bread

- 3 cups flour
- 2½ cups sugar
- 1½ cups 2% milk
- 1½ cups vegetable oil
- 3 eggs
- 1½ tablespoons poppy seeds
- 1½ teaspoons salt
- 1½ teaspoons baking powder
- 1½ teaspoons pure vanilla extract
- 1½ teaspoons pure almond extract
- 1½ teaspoons butter flavoring

Glaze

- ¾ cup powdered sugar
- ¼ cup orange juice
- ½ teaspoon butter flavoring
- ½ teaspoon pure vanilla extract
- ½ teaspoon pure almond extract

Preheat oven to 350°F.

Combine the bread ingredients in a large bowl. Mix 1 to 2 minutes with electric mixer. Pour into 2 greased 9 x 5-inch loaf pans, and bake 1 hour. Or pour into lined muffin tins and bake 30 minutes. Let cool 5 minutes.

While bread bakes, prepare glaze, mixing with a whisk (it will be runny). Pour over bread while hot. Let glaze soak in, and cool bread completely before removing from pans or covering. Freezes well.

Amaretto Cake
By Bev

Nothing says "I care" quite like this moist, melt-in-your-mouth amaretto-flavored sheet cake. We've all considered faking illness just to get one of these yummy cakes.

Cake

- 1 (16.5 ounce) Duncan Hines Classic White cake mix
- 1 cup water
- 3 egg whites
- ¼ cup vegetable oil

Glaze

- 2 tablespoons amaretto

Icing

- 4 cups powdered sugar, sifted
- ¼ cup water
- 1½ tablespoons light corn syrup
- 2 tablespoons butter, melted
- ½ teaspoon pure vanilla extract
- ¼ teaspoon pure almond extract or amaretto

Preheat oven to 350°F. Prepare cake according to package directions. Pour batter into greased-and-floured 9 x 13-inch pan.

Bake for 20 to 25 minutes or until a toothpick inserted in the center comes out clean. Cool.

Brush top of cake with amaretto. Cover with wax paper, and then seal tightly with foil or cellophane.

Place in the freezer for 2 hours to help avoid cake crumbs while icing.

Combine icing ingredients in a bowl. Blend at low speed until frosting is smooth. Spread over frozen cake. Store at room temperature.

Nanny's "Tin" Pound Cake
By Shelley

This classic Bundt cake brings back memories of grandma's kitchen. Sweet and buttery, it tastes even better the next day. Enjoy plain or topped with fresh strawberries and whipped cream.

- 2 cups sugar
- 2 sticks butter, softened
- 6 large eggs, at room temperature
- 2 cups flour
- 1½ teaspoons pure vanilla extract
- ½ teaspoon pure almond extract

Preheat oven to 350°F.

Combine sugar with softened butter. Lightly beat eggs and add to mixture. Add flour a little at a time, mix well. Add extracts and beat well. Pour into a greased-and-floured Bundt pan.

Bake for 55 to 65 minutes or until a toothpick inserted in the center comes out clean.

Cool and place in an old cookie tin or sealed cake bin overnight to lock in moisture and enhance the flavor.

Texas Hot Chocolate Cake
By Becky

Easy to make, this moist chocolate lover's delight feeds an army. We love it served with another Texas favorite, Blue Bell Homemade Vanilla ice cream.

Cake

- 2 cups flour
- 2 cups sugar
- 1 teaspoon baking soda
- ½ teaspoon cinnamon
- 2 sticks butter
- 4 tablespoons cocoa
- 1 cup water
- 2 eggs
- 1 teaspoon vanilla
- ½ cup buttermilk

Frosting

- 1 stick butter
- 4 tablespoons cocoa
- 6 tablespoons buttermilk
- 4 cups powdered sugar, sifted

Preheat oven to 350°F.

Sift flour, sugar, soda, and cinnamon together. Melt butter with cocoa and water in saucepan, bringing to a full boil. While hot, add to flour mixture and beat well. Stir in buttermilk, vanilla, and eggs until well beaten.

Pour batter into a greased, 12 x 15-inch jelly-roll pan. Bake 30 to 35 minutes or until a toothpick inserted in the center comes out clean. Frost immediately.

To make icing, bring butter, cocoa, and buttermilk to a boil in saucepan. Remove from heat. Stir chocolate mixture into sifted powdered sugar. Beat until smooth. Pour over hot cake.

Discussion Questions

1. Now that you've met the RTS girlfriends, which one do you relate to the most and why?

2. How many true friends do you have? Whom would you call for a spontaneous lunch date and an afternoon of shopping? Who would support you through a health or emotional crisis?

3. If you'd like a larger girlfriend group, list three ways you might go out of your comfort zone to meet others with similar interests. Make plans to put those ideas into action.

4. What kind of friend are you?

5. How could you be a better friend?

6. What's your idea of a fun day with girlfriends?

7. When was the last time you updated your look? We believe in constant reevaluation! Look in a full-length mirror now. What three things do you see that could be improved or updated? (Hair, makeup, clothes?)

8. List at least three things you love and appreciate about yourself. Consider both your appearance and personality.

9. If you had a chance to get away for a few days, where would you go? List names of friends you could picture traveling with you.

10. What do you want to say yes to right now? In the future? Start making plans to check these items off your "say yes" list!

11. What are your secrets to smoothing out life's panty lines?

12. What does living red thong strong mean to you?

Acknowledgments

Thank you, dear reader, for picking up our book. We hope you enjoyed meeting your new Texas besties and learning how to become red thong strong. We would be deeply honored if you'd review our book on Amazon or Goodreads. In addition, we'd love for you to connect with us on Twitter and Instagram @ RedThongStrong or at Facebook/RTSBook.

In addition to fulfilling our dreams, writing this book has made our band of sisters closer than ever. We'd like to thank everyone in the group for believing in this effort and gladly sharing both the laughs and the struggles involved in completing this ten-year ride.

We'd also like to recognize some special folks who cheered our efforts along the way. From the beginning, our precious friend and confidant Janet Aycock supported us from the sidelines. Charlotte's sweet mother, Patsy Pregeant, motivated us to keep writing even when the going got tough by publishing her first book in retirement. Courtney Mohler, the brilliant illustrator who we consider a gift from God, gave sensational style to Linda's vision for the cover. Talented author and advertising/PR expert Bob Hill, also known as Charlotte's husband, proved invaluable in brainstorming titles, editing, and planning promotions for this book.

But most importantly, we'd like to give thanks to our Lord and Savior for bringing us together, guiding us through this incredible journey, and making us forever friends.

About the Authors

Eight Texas women bound by the belief that their friendship makes life richer are behind the words of wisdom in *Red Thong Strong: Girlfriends' Little Secrets to Smoothing Life's Panty Lines*. Charlotte Hill, Linda Storer, Debbi Comparin, Becky Elder, Terri Jutras, Bev Mann, Shelley Tyler, and Debbie Williams met in a young marrieds' Sunday school class. Thirty years later, they continue to keep each other accountable, grounded, and sane.

Clockwise from top, Red Thong Strong authors Linda, Shelley, Becky, Charlotte, Bev, Terri, Debbie, and Debbi share laughs and lessons learned from more than thirty years of friendship in their first book.

Their journey together has made them experts at making, keeping, and celebrating friends. When not in writing sessions, they're serving as each other's personal stylists, planning stress-free girlfriend getaways, and hosting Pinterest-worthy parties.

These friends meet weekly to encourage, inspire, and support each other. Charlotte, Terri, Bev, Shelley, and Debbie live in Colleyville, Texas, while Linda and Debbi reside in nearby Bedford. Becky commutes to RTS meetings from her lakeside home in Whitney, Texas. This is their first book.